The Matthew Passion

To my dear sisters
Eileen and Noël

The Matthew Passion

A Lenten Journey to the Cross and Resurrection

John Fenton

The Bible Reading Fellowship

OPENING THE BIBLE

Text copyright © 1995 John Fenton

The author asserts the moral right to be
identified as the author of this work.

Published by
The Bible Reading Fellowship
Peter's Way, Sandy Lane West
Oxford OX4 5HG
ISBN 0 7459 3253 3
Albatross Books Pty Ltd
PO Box 320, Sutherland
NSW 2232, Australia
ISBN 0 7324 0947 0

First edition 1995
10 9 8 7 6 5 4 3 2 1 0

Acknowledgments
Unless otherwise stated, scripture is taken
from the Revised English Bible copyright
© 1989 by Oxford and Cambridge University
Presses.

The Revised Standard Version of the Bible
(RSV) copyright © 1946, 1952, 1971 by the
Division of Christian Education of the National
Council of the Churches of Christ in the USA.

A catalogue record for this book is
available from the British Library

Printed and bound in Great Britain
by Biddles Ltd, Guildford and King's Lynn

Contents

Preface

My thanks are due to the Oxford University Press for permission to print the text of The Revised English Bible (1989), and to Michael Goulder and the S.P.C.K. for allowing me to include the poem in Appendix III. I must also thank Shelagh Brown and Andrew Starkie of the Bible Reading Fellowship for their help throughout the writing of this book, and my wife who typed it from a manuscript that was seldom legible.

John Fenton
Oxford
Feast of Saint Benedict 1995

Introduction

The principal aim of this book is to provide the reader with something to think about every day from Ash Wednesday to Easter Day. For each of these days there is a passage from Matthew's Gospel, some reflections on it and some suggestions for prayer that might arise out of the reading. Though it is intended to be a book for Lent, there is no reason why it might not be used at any other time of the year, either taking one passage each day or reading it straight through, however one found it helpful.

Some explanation of the arrangement of the material from Matthew may be useful at this point. The account of the passion of Christ (in Matthew 26 and 27) provides the readings for the weekdays in the second half of Lent, from the Monday after the fourth Sunday in Lent to the Saturday before Easter Day, inclusive. These passages are taken in the order in which they come in Matthew, and without any omissions. The reading for Easter Day itself is the whole of Matthew's final chapter, 28. In the earlier part of Lent, there is a selection of passages from Matthew 1–25 on the weekdays, arranged in the order in which they stand in the Gospel, but on the Sundays there is a different scheme. Each Sunday, from the first in Lent to Palm Sunday, there is a passage which is either one of Matthew's miracle stories or is in some way concerned with miracles. This is because Sundays in Lent are not part of the forty days; it seemed right, therefore, to mark this by having a different arrangement of readings. Every Sunday is a reminder of the resurrection of Christ; that is why the readings are some of the miracle stories.

From this it will be apparent that this book is about another book; it is about the Gospel that is now printed at the beginning of the New Testament in all copies of the Bible. The intention of the present writer is to point to what may be seen in Matthew, with the hope that, by doing so, Matthew's Gospel will become clearer and the wealth that it contains more accessible. It therefore goes without saying that if the reader of this book does not find that Matthew's Gospel is being illuminated, there is no reason at all for proceeding with it any further.

There are, in fact, three levels of activity that are easily distinguishable when reading this book: first, reading this book itself; secondly, reading Matthew's Gospel; thirdly, believing in Christ and in his words and deeds. The third is by far the most important and provides the criterion for assessing the other two. Reading Matthew has helped many people in the past to believe in Christ and it has been the most popular of all the Gospels.

Because this is in the first instance a Lent book, it concentrates on the last three chapters of Matthew (26–28) and omits many passages from chapters 1 to 25, selecting a few most relevant to the theme: *The Matthew Passion*. To treat a book like Matthew's in this way is to violate the intentions of the author. Writers of books that contain a narrative do not want their readers to be selective; they would not have included anything that they thought optional or irrelevant. It is different with those who compile dictionaries, telephone directories or railway timetables: they know that no one with any sanity will read them through from beginning to end. Gospels are not like that, and the evangelists who wrote them presumably expected them to be read straight through: it is only in this way that the reader will appreciate the books in their totality.

One way the peril of selectivity can be mitigated is if the reader takes time to read Matthew from 1:1 to 28:20, preferably at a single sitting (it might take two hours) and if possible more than once. Matthew's book is the clearest of the four Gospels in the arrangement and organization of its material. He has made his purpose clear through the structure that he has given to the book, and this structure stands out for the reader to see it and take note of it. Matthew's Gospel is like a building in the eighteenth-century classical style: anyone can see its symmetry and proportion.

The way in which Matthew draws attention to the shape of his book is by the repetition of a formula: the same set of words, occuring five times altogether, marks off five points in the book where Jesus stops talking and the story moves on. The first instance is at the end of the Sermon on the Mount: 'When Jesus had finished this discourse the people were amazed at his teaching' (7:28; the other passages are 11:1; 13:53; 19:1 and 26:1). The formula signals the end of the speech; the collecting of an audience marks the beginning of it, and the result is that Matthew has given us the main teaching of Jesus in his Gospel set out in five clearly indicated sections: 5–7; 10:5–42; 13:3–52; 18:3–35; 23:2—25:46.

Another device that Matthew frequently uses is the mirror image: ABC...CBA. He has arranged the five speeches so that the two longest are first and last, the two shortest second and fourth, and the third speech is divided by a change of scene: 'Then he sent the people away, and went into the house' (13:36). (See Appendix I, page 151.)

Matthew has used the structure, or shape, of the book to carry a story that develops as one reads it. Jesus proclaims the coming of God's rule in chapter 4; he teaches his disciples what sort of people they must be to enter this age in chapters 5–7; he then heals sick people in chapters 8 and 9, and this is evidence for the coming total defeat of Satan and routing of all opposition to God. In chapter 10 the twelve apostles are sent out to proclaim the same message of the coming rule of God, and to demonstrate it by healing; and they are to do this only to the lost sheep of the house of Israel—not to Gentiles, not to Samaritans. In chapters 11 and 12 Matthew collects material to show how this generation of Israel has rejected John the Baptist and Jesus. Then, in chapter 13, parables explain why it is so: not all seeds that are sown bear fruit; there are weeds as well as wheat; there are different kinds of fish caught in a net, and some are good but others are useless. By now we are in the middle of the book, where Jesus turns from the crowds to the disciples—the future lies with them, and with the Gentiles. They will replace Jews as the tenants of the vineyard, and after his death and resurrection Jesus sends the Eleven to all the nations, to make disciples of them.

The turning-point of the plot of the book is also the middle-point of the structure (13:36); what was offered first to the Jews is now to be offered to Gentiles (see Appendix II, page 152).

Every student of the New Testament knows that the first three Gospels (Matthew, Mark and Luke) are both similar to one another and yet also different from each other. They are different because each of them is the work of a different author who had his own vocabulary, his own style of writing and his own ideas and purposes. Nothing has obliterated the characteristics that distinguish one author from the others. (To give one example of this, a Greek word that means 'then' is used six times by Mark, fifteen times by Luke, but ninety-one times by Matthew; it is a characteristic mark of his style.) What is more of a problem is why these three Gospels are so similar to each other: we expect diversity, because people are like that; we are surprised by agreement, because people do not usually tell the same story in almost identical words. In these three Gospels, however, there are places where the same words come in the same order in two or three of the books. The only explanation of this that is satisfactory is that there is dependence at the literary level— either that the authors wrote what was in documents that are now lost, or that they wrote what they read in another Gospel still extant.

The problem has been studied for 200 years, and the solution that is most commonly held is that Mark, the shortest Gospel, is the oldest, and that Matthew knew the book in the form in which we have it (in Greek), except that it finished at Mark 16:8. He will have incorporated almost all of Mark in his Gospel, keeping the Marcan paragraphs in the same order in Matthew 13:53—28:20 (apart from one rearrangement) but changing the order in the first half of his book to create the plan and plot that we have already noticed. This is the hypothesis that will be used in this book. We shall notice, every so often, that Matthew is different from Mark, or that he is identical with Mark, assuming in both cases that Mark is the source from which Matthew has derived more than half of his book.

Three points follow from this. The first is that this way of explaining the relationship between Matthew and Mark is not the way in which it was explained through the greater part of Church history: from the fourth century to the nineteenth the belief was that Matthew was the earlier Gospel, and Mark was a summary of it. The second point is that this reversal of the supposed order of writing of these books has had the effect of making Mark the more popular Gospel than Matthew. The pioneer, the man who first thought of writing a Gospel, inevitably takes precedence over the man who used his material, edited it and added some more. The third consequence of the change of order is that it is now very hard to think that Matthew's Gospel is by the apostle Matthew, one of the Twelve, whose name appears in all the lists in the New Testament (Matthew 10:3; Mark 3:18; Luke 6:15 and Acts 1:13). Would a person who had been there when most of the things described in his book had happened have been so dependent on the account given by someone who had not been there? Do the changes made between Mark and Matthew indicate the recollection of a participant? Matthew's book never claims to be by an apostle (except in the title). (In common usage, the names Matthew, Mark, Luke and John continue to be used to refer both to the books and to the authors of the books, without implying that these were in fact the names of the four writers; and this practice is followed here also.)

This brings us to the question of when the books were written, and unfortunately there is no generally agreed answer. Most writers date Mark either shortly before or shortly after AD70; that would then be the earliest possible date for Matthew (on the theory that he used Mark). The latest possible date is the time of Ignatius of Antioch who wrote letters about AD110 that seem to presuppose knowledge of Matthew.

Customs and procedures in all departments of life were different in the ancient world from what they are in ours. We should find it not only strange but reprehensible if a writer were to incorporate nine-tenths of a book by a previous author in his own work without ever mentioning the fact. Nevertheless, that is what seems to have happened here, and apparently it would not have surprised people at the time: conventions were different; there were no quotation marks or footnotes; even the idea of authorship would not have been the same as ours, and the method of writing about the past that these evangelists used was quite different from the way people would set about it today. Another formula that Matthew uses illustrates the point. It comes only in this Gospel, and we meet it frequently in the first two chapters—'All this happened in order to fulfil what the Lord declared through the prophet...' (1:22). Matthew believed that God had told the Hebrews of the eighth and seventh centuries BC what would happen in the first century AD: the virgin birth of Jesus, the return of the holy family from Egypt, the settlement in Nazareth, details of the treachery of Judas Iscariot, and so on. But, as we shall see, it goes further than that. Matthew corrects and supplements the information he has from Mark by reading the (Old Testament) scriptures: the wine that Jesus was offered at the crucifixion was mixed with gall, because the Psalmist said so; children greeted Jesus as Son of David because of something in another Psalm. Familiarity with the Gospels sometimes conceals from us the strangeness of the writers' minds: they were men of the ancient world, in many ways not like us.

One thread that runs through Matthew's book that will certainly make us feel uncomfortable is his anti-Jewishness. As we have seen already, the plot of the Gospel is: how the good news was rejected by the Jews in order to be sent to the Gentiles. A Jew himself, Matthew had left the synagogue to be a follower of Jesus, and he seems to have been always aware of this break in his own life and the alienation that it had created with his non-Christian contemporaries. This is perhaps the most troublesome feature of this Gospel, for us who live in the century of the Holocaust.

But there is another element in this book that can also contribute to the decline in its popularity at this time. Another Matthean formula encapsulates it: '...where there will be wailing and grinding of teeth'. Matthew has it six times, Luke once, and it does not appear anywhere else in the New Testament. There is more about judgment, condemnation, hell and torment in Matthew than in all the rest of the Gospels taken together—and this is not endearing to us, though we know that it was popular at various times with our predecessors.

On the other hand, there is one theme that runs through Matthew's Gospel that does appeal to some late-twentieth-century readers. The book could be described as a celebration of weakness. The authority of Jesus is the authority of one who has been tried by the chief priests and elders and condemned as a blasphemer. The mock sceptre that is given by the soldiers is used to beat him about his head: his power is his refusal to use power, but to suffer instead. He does not appeal to the Father for the help of the angels, though he could; scripture would not be fulfilled if he did. He is the one who is gentle and humble-hearted, and he requires his followers also to be poor in spirit, sorrowful, gentle, hungry and thirsty, merciful and persecuted. By 'gentle' is meant the opposite of pushy, thrusting, self-confident. At the beginning we see the contrast between King Herod, the chief priests and scribes on the one side, and Joseph, Mary and the baby conceived out of wedlock on the other side. At the end of the book we see how no amount of sealing the stone or mounting the guard can keep the dead man in. He continues to suffer with his followers who are hungry, thirsty, away from home, naked, sick and in prison; they and he depend on those who do not know who they are for their sustenance and consolation. He even relates to his followers as their food and drink, being destroyed by them in order that they may live.

It is easy to miss this strand in Matthew's book; there is so much else that we can lose sight of it. Matthew knew what it was to be mocked by those whom he had previously thought learned, and to be insulted by those who had status and pre-eminence in their society. This is why it is wise to read Matthew with the theme of Christ's passion as our guide: his Gospel celebrates those things that our society often values least.

My thoughts are not your thoughts

Matthew 1:1–17

*The genealogy of Jesus Christ, son of David, son of Abraham.
Abraham was the father of Isaac, Isaac of Jacob, Jacob of
Judah and his brothers, Judah of Perez and Zarah (their
mother was Tamar), Perez of Hezron, Hezron of Ram, Ram of
Amminadab, Amminadab of Nahshon, Nahshon of Salmon,
Salmon of Boaz (his mother was Rahab), Boaz of Obed (his
mother was Ruth), Obed of Jesse; and Jesse was the father of
King David.*

*David was the father of Solomon (his mother had been the
wife of Uriah), Solomon of Rehoboam, Rehoboam of Abijah,
Abijah of Asa, Asa of Jehoshaphat, Jehoshaphat of Joram,
Joram of Uzziah, Uzziah of Jotham, Jotham of Ahaz, Ahaz of
Hezekiah, Hezekiah of Manasseh, Manasseh of Amon, Amon
of Josiah; and Josiah was the father of Jeconiah and his
brothers at the time of the deportation to Babylon.*

*After the deportation Jeconiah was the father of Shealtiel,
Shealtiel of Zerubbabel, Zerubbabel of Abiud, Abiud of Eliakim,
Eliakim of Azor, Azor of Zadok, Zadok of Achim, Achim of
Eliud, Eliud of Eleazar, Eleazar of Matthan, Matthan of Jacob,*

Jacob of Joseph, the husband of Mary, who gave birth to Jesus called Messiah.

There were thus fourteen generations in all from Abraham to David, fourteen from David until the deportation to Babylon, and fourteen from the deportation until the Messiah.

It would be tempting to skip the beginning of Matthew's book, the genealogy of Jesus. If we did so, however, we should miss an important clue that Matthew provides for understanding his Gospel on the very first page. He has taken many of the names of the ancestors of Jesus from the early chapters of Chronicles. Chronicles, like Matthew's Gospel, begins with a list of names and ends with instructions being given by one who has authority (compare Matthew 28:18–20 with 2 Chronicles 36:23). Matthew wanted his readers to believe, just as the writer of Chronicles wanted his readers to believe, that what he was describing were events of great importance: God was at work, creating the community to which the readers belonged.

Matthew detects a pattern in the events of the past: there were fourteen generations from the beginning of Israelite history in Abraham to David, the first king who lived in Jerusalem; then there were another fourteen generations from David to the deportation— that is, the exile; and a third fourteen from the deportation until Christ, given his authority after the resurrection. He is David's son, the beginning of the new age.

Alongside this there is a further idea, which at first looks like a complete contradiction of it. God is at work, but in a most unexpected way. Matthew refers to five women in the genealogy: Tamar; Rahab; Ruth; the wife of Uriah; and Mary, the mother of Jesus. There was something unusual about each of them: Tamar was the daughter-in-law of Judah (who was the father of her children); Rahab was a harlot; Ruth was not an Israelite but a Moabitess; Bathsheba (her name is not given) was the wife of Uriah with whom David committed adultery; and Mary conceived Jesus before she was married to Joseph, as Matthew will go on to explain.

God is not like us, and his ways are different from ours. He did not preserve the royal line of Judah from irregularities, and Matthew deliberately draws our attention to them by mentioning these women. We cannot determine in advance how God will act, except to say that we must expect surprises. (See Appendix III, page 153)

Matthew will tell us both that scripture was fulfilled in the life and death and resurrection of Jesus, and that these events were unexpected and unrecognized by those who knew the scriptures best. God works in what seem to us ungodly ways.

Let us not think that we know.
Stop us from being dogmatic.
Keep us open to the facts, especially when they are
    unwelcome.

Thursday

God with us

Matthew 1:18–25

This is how the birth of Jesus Christ came about. His mother Mary was betrothed to Joseph; before their marriage she found she was going to have a child through the Holy Spirit. Being a man of principle, and at the same time wanting to save her from exposure, Joseph made up his mind to have the marriage contract quietly set aside. He had resolved on this, when an angel of the Lord appeared to him in a dream and said, 'Joseph, son of David, do not be afraid to take Mary home with you to be your wife. It is through the Holy Spirit that she has conceived. She will bear a son; and you shall give him the name Jesus, for he will save his people from their sins.' All this happened in order to fulfil what the Lord declared through the prophet: 'A virgin will conceive and bear a son, and he shall be called Emmanuel,' a name which means 'God is with us'. When he woke Joseph did as the angel of the Lord had directed him; he took Mary home to be his wife, but had no intercourse with her until her son was born. And he named the child Jesus.

Matthew has led us to expect there to be something unusual in the circumstances surrounding the birth of Jesus. On all the other occasions when a woman was mentioned in the genealogy there had been irregularity. How will it be in the case of Joseph and Mary?

As far as we know, this is probably the earliest account that we have of the birth of Jesus; Mark, the first evangelist (as is now thought), had begun with the baptism of Jesus when he was an adult. Luke is the only other writer in the New Testament who describes Jesus' early years, and his account differs from Matthew's on some points; but they both agree that Jesus was conceived by the Holy Spirit. Matthew tells his story from the point of view of Joseph (Luke from that of Mary). Joseph is caught between two stools: should he release Mary from betrothal because she is pregnant before marriage (presumably, he will think, by another man) or should he go ahead to save her embarrassment? He decides on the former, but is told by an angel in a dream to do the latter: Mary has not been unfaithful, and the child to which she will give birth is to be the agent of God for the salvation of his people. God's promise through Isaiah (7:14) will be fulfilled and Jesus will be Emmanuel, God with us.

We have here in Matthew the first of eleven instances where he introduces a quotation from the Old Testament to show that what happened in the recent past fulfilled what God had predicted through the Hebrew prophets centuries before. No doubt Matthew's purpose is to persuade unbelievers to believe and to reprove those who do not; but he also wants to convince the believers of the great things that God has done for them.

None of the titles that had been in use in Israel before this time would be capable of describing what was to be believed about Jesus; they would all leave something unsaid. He was a prophet, but more than a prophet. He was a king, a son of David, but his authority was more than David's. He was a wise man, but he had greater wisdom than Solomon. He was a saviour, but his salvation exceeded that achieved by his namesake, Joshua the son of Nun.

Matthew uses the expression 'the Son of God'. It had been used before, of the whole nation, of holy men and of kings. Now, however, it was to be used in a new way, meaning that God would deal with his creation finally through Jesus. His is the last name in the list that begins with Abraham, and there cannot be any more because he has done all that needs to be done. He is the climax of the series of God's agents, the one who will never need to be replaced because he is alive for ever, and with us always. Notice how the first quotation from prophesy matches the final words of Jesus in the book: 'I will be with you always, to the end of time' (28:20).

Increase our faith.
Break down our opposition. — even when it is subconscious
Persuade us of your goodness towards us.

This we can know in our minds
+ not in our hearts.

He who is not with me is against me

Matthew 2:1–6, 16–18

Jesus was born at Bethlehem in Judaea during the reign of Herod. After his birth astrologers from the east arrived in Jerusalem, asking, 'Where is the new-born king of the Jews? We observed the rising of his star, and we have come to pay him homage.' King Herod was greatly perturbed when he heard this, and so was the whole of Jerusalem. He called together the chief priests and scribes of the Jews, and asked them where the Messiah was to be born. 'At Bethlehem in Judaea,' they replied, 'for this is what the prophet wrote: "Bethlehem in the land of Judah, you are by no means least among the rulers of Judah; for out of you shall come a ruler to be the shepherd of my people Israel." '…

When Herod realized that the astrologers had tricked him he flew into a rage, and gave orders for the massacre of all the boys aged two years or under, in Bethlehem and throughout the whole district, in accordance with the time he had ascertained from the astrologers. So the words spoken through Jeremiah the prophet were fulfilled: 'A voice was heard in Rama, sobbing in bitter grief; it was Rachel weeping for her children, and refusing to be comforted, because they were no more.'

Matthew's way of describing God's purpose is to say that he will rule over everything that he has made, both in heaven and on earth. The Jews believed that God had given temporary authority to emperors and kings, and that rulers frequently misused it, not recognizing that governance was a gift from God. (The first seven chapters of Daniel are a study of this theme.) Rulers who did not obey God persecuted God's people; it had been so in Egypt at the time of Moses, and in Babylon during the exile.

Herod the Great, who ruled from 37–4BC, is presented by Matthew as a king in the tradition of wicked rulers. Herod and Jesus are alternatives, incompatible: neutrality and comprehensiveness are out of the question. No one could be subject to both of them.

The astrologers from the east represent all those who are 'with' Jesus, while Herod and the whole of Jerusalem stand for those who are 'against' him. The former worship him and offer him their gifts; the latter seek to destroy him.

In the story of the exodus, Moses had fled from Egypt for safety and then returned there to lead God's people out to the Promised Land. In Matthew's account of the childhood of Jesus, everything is reversed: Egypt is the place of safety to which he is taken, in order to return later to the place of danger and destruction. Judea now stands for unbelief. Herod is outwitted by the astrologers, but this only postpones the outcome; eventually the forces of evil will rally and Jesus will be destroyed at their hands.

In these introductory chapters, Matthew is preparing his readers for all that is to come as we read the rest of his book. The arrival of the astrologers prepares us for one of Matthew's major themes: the contrast between unbelieving Jews and believing Gentiles. The astrologers are to be understood as representatives of those who were not born in Judaism; they ask for the new-born king of the Jews. Matthew is observing the convention that Jews speak of themselves as Israelites, whereas Gentiles call them Jews. (See

27:37 and 41–42, where the same distinction is made.) Gentiles, therefore, have come to worship, led by a star; Jews attempt to destroy. Matthew himself was almost certainly a Jew who had become a convert to the followers of Jesus; and at the time when he was writing the Gospel, the division between unbelieving Jews and Christians had become bitter and violent. It is apparent all through Matthew's book.

One way to deal with this feature of Matthew's Gospel is to resist the temptation to identify certain classes of person as if they were irredeemably wicked. That way lies racism, sexism and many other politically incorrect 'isms'. It is individuals who make choices, and the line that divides being for Christ from being against him runs through everybody; it is internal, not external. Moreover, the sorting of wheat from tares is not our affair, but must be left to those whose proper business it is.

Stop us from deceiving ourselves.
Let us have no false self-confidence.
Faith saves, and nothing else.

John the Baptist

Matthew 3:1–12

In the course of time John the Baptist appeared in the Judaean wilderness, proclaiming this message: 'Repent, for the kingdom of Heaven is upon you!' It was of him that the prophet Isaiah spoke when he said,

> *A voice cries in the wilderness,*
> *'Prepare the way for the Lord;*
> *clear a straight path for him.'*

John's clothing was a rough coat of camel's hair, with a leather belt round his waist, and his food was locusts and wild honey. Everyone flocked to him from Jerusalem, Judaea, and the Jordan valley, and they were baptized by him in the river Jordan, confessing their sins.

When he saw many of the Pharisees and Sadducees coming for baptism he said to them: 'Vipers' brood! Who warned you to escape from the wrath that is to come? Prove your repentance by the fruit you bear; and do not imagine you can say, "We have Abraham for our father." I tell you that God can make children for Abraham out of these stones. The axe lies ready at the roots of the trees; every tree that fails to produce good fruit is cut down and thrown on the fire. I baptize you with water, for repentance; but the one who comes after me is mightier than I am, whose sandals I am not worthy to remove. He will baptize you with the Holy Spirit and with fire. His winnowing-shovel is ready in his hand and he will clear his threshing-floor; he will gather the wheat into his granary, but the chaff he will burn on a fire that can never be put out.'

John the Baptist is present in all four Gospels near the beginning. There is no doubt that this is partly due to the fact that Jesus was a follower of John and was baptized by him; some of Jesus' disciples may also have been disciples of the Baptist. The contemporaries of John and Jesus would have seen the followers of Jesus as a group within the larger Baptist movement, sharing many of the same ideas with them. John, like Jesus, proclaimed the coming of the kingdom of heaven. (Matthew almost always has 'of Heaven', but the other Gospels always have 'the kingdom of God'. Both expressions mean the same: 'heaven' was simply a devout way of avoiding saying 'God'; compare 'good heavens' and 'heaven help us'.) The meaning of the expression is to be found in, for example, Daniel, the last book of the Old Testament to be written, and therefore the nearest in time to the Gospels: after the four world empires of the Babylonians, Medes, Persians and Greeks, God himself will take over and Israel will be his agent.

But before this could happen, they believed, God would sort out the wicked from the good, as in a harvest; there would be destruction for the 'chaff' but life in the age to come for the 'wheat'. John lays great stress on repentance, change of mind showing itself in change of performance. 'Fruit' stands for deeds, and deeds speak louder than words.

Notice in particular that it is religious people that John attacks most severely, Pharisees and Sadducees. Sadducees were the families of the priests in the temple, and lived largely in Jerusalem and its environs; Pharisees were laymen who kept the rules of holiness as they applied to the priests, while earning a living in the world. The modern equivalent would be the associates of a religious community of monks or nuns, or third order of friars. Religious observance by itself does not displace faith, but it may appear to do so; that is the hazard.

John mentions reliance upon external and fortuitous circumstances: 'We have Abraham for our father.' Membership of the nation will no longer be significant because faith will replace racial status, and be the only means of salvation. Faith of this kind is a possibility for everybody whatever their race; it abolishes the distinction between Jews and Gentiles. God can and will create children of Abraham out of stones: Gentiles will become believers, and they will be the Israel of God.

The Baptist demands fruit—good fruit, the fruit that is appropriate to those who have changed their minds because they believe that God is about to rule. John is not more specific, nor does he need to be, because he bears witness to another man who comes after him and is far more important than he. Jesus will take up what John has foretold and fill in the content that he has outlined.

Let us not forget the Baptist, than whom there has been none greater.
He tells us what we do not want to hear: 'Repent. Bear fruit.'
Make us attend to him.

Jesus the healer

Matthew 8:5–13

As Jesus entered Capernaum a centurion came up to ask his help. 'Sir,' he said, 'my servant is lying at home paralysed and racked with pain.' Jesus said, 'I will come and cure him.' But the centurion replied, 'Sir, I am not worthy to have you under my roof. You need only say the word and my servant will be cured. I know, for I am myself under orders, with soldiers under me. I say to one, "Go," and he goes; to another, "Come here," and he comes; and to my servant, "Do this," and he does it.' Jesus heard him with astonishment, and said to the people who were following him, 'Truly I tell you: nowhere in Israel have I found such faith. Many, I tell you, will come from east and west to sit with Abraham, Isaac, and Jacob at the banquet in the kingdom of Heaven. But those who were born to the kingdom will be thrown out into the dark, where there will be wailing and grinding of teeth.' Then Jesus said to the centurion, 'Go home; as you have believed, so let it be.' At that very moment the boy recovered.

John the Baptist and Jesus both proclaimed the coming of God's kingdom, the time when God would rule and no one else. We do not know whether the Baptist performed miracles: none is recorded, and in John's Gospel it is said that he did not (10:41). All the Gospels agree, however, that Jesus healed people; and not only that, but, according to Matthew, Mark and Luke, he sent his disciples on a mission to preach and heal.

Preaching, in this context, means declaring that God will rule, and healing is evidence that this is so. Many illnesses were thought to be the work of evil spirits; their time was coming to an end because one who was greater had arrived. When God ruled, there would be no more sickness because there would be no more evil. To believe in Jesus as healer was to believe in him as the one through whom God will reign.

Mark's Gospel has a greater concentration of stories of healings and other miracles than any of the other three; it is the shortest of the four, and the ratio of miracles to pages is highest in it. Matthew, in his much longer book, has reproduced them all (though sometimes combining two into one story) but added only a few that were not in Mark. This story of the centurion and his servant is one that was not in Mark, but it has many features that made it attractive to Matthew: there is the contrast between Jews and Gentiles; emphasis on the authority of Jesus, who heals by his word; and the first of six instances of the formula, 'where there will be wailing and grinding of teeth'.

The centurion sees Jesus as someone who is like himself: under authority, but able to exercise authority and effect obedience in others. He expects his commands to be obeyed, and he believes that what Jesus says will also produce results. Jesus, therefore, can cure his servant who is paralysed and racked with pain.

Jesus says that this is the faith that is needed to enter the kingdom of heaven; he has not found it in Israel, but here it is in a Gentile. Gentiles who believe will join in the banquet of the age to come; those who were expected to enter (the unbelieving Jews) will not. (Compare 3:9, where the Baptist says: 'Do not imagine you can say, "We have Abraham for our father." I tell you that God can make children for Abraham out of these stones.')

The coming of the kingdom is good news because it is about healing: what paralyses us will be removed, and what makes us suffer will be abolished. Jesus preaches and demonstrates this by his words and his deeds. The healing miracles are good-news stories because they encapsulate the whole purpose of Jesus, which is to bring release, freedom, life and joy to the world.

What is particularly noteworthy about the centurion's faith is that he has seen the relationship between being under the authority of another and having the authority that is effective. Jesus is the healer because he is obedient to the will of his Father. His power to heal cannot be detached from his relationship with God. Power that is detached is demonic. The dependence of Jesus on the Father will finally be demonstrated in his resurrection from the dead.

Thank you for the obedience of Christ.
Thank you for the healing of all ills.
Thank you for those who have faith.

Does Jesus support the Centurion's view of authority? It is not explicit that he does.

John baptizes Jesus

Matthew 3:13-17

Then Jesus arrived at the Jordan from Galilee, and came to John to be baptized by him. John tried to dissuade him. 'Do you come to me?' he said. 'It is I who need to be baptized by you.' Jesus replied, 'Let it be so for the present; it is right for us to do all that God requires.' Then John allowed him to come. No sooner had Jesus been baptized and come up out of the water than the heavens were opened and he saw the Spirit of God descending like a dove to alight on him. And there came a voice from heaven saying, 'This is my beloved Son, in whom I take delight.'

As far as we know, the followers of Jesus have always believed him to have been without fault; the one who saves his people from their sins could not have been a sinner himself. But John's baptism in the Jordan had been for repentance, and those who were baptized by him had confessed their sins. How was it possible to relate the fact that Jesus had been not only a follower of John, but also one who was baptized by him, to the Christian understanding of Jesus? How did it happen that the sinless one was baptized for repentance?

Mark was unaware of the problem, or else he ignored it; but Matthew saw the need for an explanation. He has added the conversation between John and Jesus: John says that he needs to be baptized by Jesus, and Jesus replies that it is right for them to do all that God requires. So Matthew's explanation of why the one who was without sin was baptized is because Jesus obeyed God and that he believed that this was God's will for him.

The baptism of Jesus is the beginning of his public ministry, and it is important because it corrects a mistake that the readers of Matthew's book could easily make. He has told us that Jesus is the Messiah, descended from Judah in the royal line; that he was miraculously conceived, called Jesus because he will save his people from their sins, divinely protected from the malice of Herod. All of this might have led us to think of Jesus as a strong, powerful and victorious leader—like David, only greater. (Matthew will, in fact, apply the title 'Son of David' to Jesus eight times—more frequently than any other Gospel writer.)

If Matthew had given us no further information about Jesus beyond his power and authority we should have found the rest of his book impossible to understand. How could such a person come to be condemned, mocked and crucified? Surely that would make him a failure? There was no precedent for a king being honoured because of rejection and death.

The mistake would lie in applying our criteria to Jesus and thinking about him in the way we think about great people: politicians, leaders, benefactors, inventors and so on. We know how to assess success in these cases.

Matthew believes that Jesus must be understood in a different way. His 'success' (if we may use the word) lay in his obedience to the Father, in doing the Father's will. The Father's will for Jesus was only known as it was lived, and as it, eventually, led him to his death.

According to Matthew, Jesus believed that John the Baptist was a prophet, and more than a prophet (11:9). If John called people to be baptized, Jesus believed that he must be baptized also; he could not stand apart from the other followers of John. Not to get into the water would be to resist the Father's will.

Baptism was thought of as an enacted death and resurrection (see Romans 6:3–4)—the waters of destruction overwhelmed you, and you rose into a new life. To be God's Son is to delight God by obedience to him, as the voice from heaven declared—even if it means death.

Every day: what do you want me to do?
It does not matter whether it is attractive, fulfilling,
*   satisfying.*
For Jesus, life was obedience, from start to finish.

The devil tempts Jesus

Matthew 4:1–11

Jesus was then led by the Spirit into the wilderness, to be tempted by the devil. For forty days and nights he fasted, and at the end of them he was famished. The tempter approached him and said, 'If you are the Son of God, tell these stones to become bread.' Jesus answered, 'Scripture says, "Man is not to live on bread alone, but on every word that comes from the mouth of God."'

The devil then took him to the Holy City and set him on the parapet of the temple. 'If you are the Son of God,' he said, 'throw yourself down; for scripture says, "He will put his angels in charge of you, and they will support you in their arms, for fear you should strike your foot against a stone."' Jesus answered him, 'Scripture also says, "You are not to put the Lord your God to the test."'

The devil took him next to a very high mountain, and showed him all the kingdoms of the world in their glory. 'All these', he said, 'I will give you, if you will only fall down and do me homage.' But Jesus said, 'Out of my sight, Satan! Scripture says, "You shall do homage to the Lord your God and worship him alone."'

Then the devil left him; and angels came and attended to his needs.

There is a sense of inevitability about Matthew's account of the temptations of Jesus. The narrative flows on in a continuous logical sequence, each new step developing out of the one before.

God has spoken and said that Jesus is his beloved Son in whom he takes delight. But to be God's Son means to do his will, and this has to be learnt in practice, like any other kind of performance. Obedience can only be exercised in the face of the possibility of disobedience; it would not be obedience if it was the result of programming.

Israel, God's son, came out of Egypt (Hosea 11:1, quoted at Matthew 2:15) and spent forty years in the wilderness; Jesus also goes into the wilderness and is there for forty days and forty nights. Israel was hungry and complained, and God fed them with manna; Jesus is hungry. The Baptist had said that God could make Israelites out of stones, so he could do the lighter task of making bread from stones to feed his Son. But Israel's hunger had been to teach them that they must rely on God: this is how Jesus resists the first temptation.

If it is on God that Jesus must rely, and on every word that comes from his mouth, then there is a Psalm (91) in which God promises to care for those who trust him; his angels will lift them up. The second temptation therefore is to put this faith into practice by giving God the opportunity to demonstrate that he can be relied on. Israel had tempted God at Massah but Jesus will not put God to the test.

If Jesus is not to be caught out by false beliefs about God and perverted interpretations of scripture, then why not face the facts? The devil is *de facto* god of the world; he and his minions rule it, and exercise power through emperors and kings. If Jesus is to be the ruler of the world—the tempter says—the quickest way for him to achieve that end will be for him to do homage to the devil. Israel had worshipped the metal bull-calf, but Jesus will not worship the devil. He is to be the ruler of the world, he will come as judge and sit on his glorious throne (25:31), but only when God wills it to happen. Meanwhile he must walk in faith.

Matthew will return to those themes when he is describing the crucifixion in chapter 27; again, the title Son of God will be used, and miracles will be asked for, to demonstrate who Jesus is. But he will not listen: this is not the way of obedience to the Father's will, and this is not the proper fulfilment of the scriptures (26:53–54).

Obedience involves faith and hope, and these provide little, if any, consolation in the present. Jesus comes out of the temptations with nothing: no bread, no proof of God's care for him, no assurance that the kingdoms of the world in their glory will be his. Faith and hope postpone both evidence and rewards to the future, when God decides to act. Then, and only then, will he send his angels to attend to our needs. For Jesus, as the passion narrative will show, this will happen only *post mortem*.

Teach us to walk by faith, not by sight.
Help us to do without reassurance and success.
Let the darkness be light enough.

Membership of the kingdom

Matthew 5:3–10

'Blessed are the poor in spirit;
the kingdom of Heaven is theirs.
Blessed are the sorrowful;
they shall find consolation.
Blessed are the gentle;
they shall have the earth for their possession.
Blessed are those who hunger and thirst to see
right prevail;
they shall be satisfied.
Blessed are those who show mercy;
mercy shall be shown to them.
Blessed are those whose hearts are pure;
they shall see God.
Blessed are the peacemakers;
they shall be called God's children.
Blessed are those who are persecuted in the
cause of right;
the kingdom of Heaven is theirs.'

Already in Matthew's book, both John the Baptist and Jesus have told us that God is going to rule and that entry into this new era calls for a change of mind; but neither Jesus nor John has said what the character of the citizens of the kingdom must be. Chapters 5–7 will deal with this.

This whole section is known traditionally as the Sermon on the Mount, and it is introduced by eight short sayings, called beatitudes (from the Latin *beatus*, blessed). Matthew—who is always a careful writer, attending to detail at every point—seems to have paid extremely close attention to these eight sayings, arranging them so that they stand out as a summary of what is to follow and will be easy to remember.

Each beatitude consists of two parts: first, a statement that a certain sort of person (poor, sorrowful and so on) is blessed; then an explanation of why this is so (in Greek, introduced by the word 'because', for example, '... because the kingdom of Heaven is theirs').

The explanations, in the second part of each beatitude, are all descriptions of how it will be for the blessed when the new age begins: they will share God's rule by reigning with him on the earth; they will be consoled and join in the feast; God will have been merciful to them at the judgment; they will see God and he will declare them his children. The explanation in the eighth beatitude repeats what was said in the first: 'the kingdom of Heaven is theirs'. This rounds the list off by returning to the beginning.

All seven explanations are in effect promises of the one reward in the future: to be a member of the kingdom of heaven. It is not possible to pick and choose between them, as though one were to say one was interested in being shown mercy, but not in seeing God. All those who will be blessed will receive all the promises in the second parts of the beatitudes.

The emphasis in the beatitudes is on what is said in the first part of each of them. A theme that runs through the first four is the contrast between now and then: the poor will be rich; the sorrowful will be comforted; the downtrodden will rule; the hungry will be fed. Then there is a change of tone, with greater emphasis on the action of God: he will forgive those who have forgiven others; he will be seen by those who are single-minded; he will acknowledge the peacemakers as his children; he will promote those who have been persecuted.

When God takes over from the devil as the ruler of the world everything will be different: what works now will not work then; and what does not pay now will be all that matters then. This is why there must be repentance, change of mind: those who will enter the kingdom must live by its ways in the present and suffer for doing so.

In the passion narrative, Matthew will tell us that Jesus is the king and that his kingship will be seen in his persecution, humiliation and death. The way of the king is to be the way of his subjects also. This was so important to Matthew that he put it at the beginning of the teaching of Jesus.

Overturn our ideas of what matters.
Detach us from the world, the flesh and the devil.
Make us long to see right prevail.

The Lord's Prayer

Matthew 6:9-13

'This is how you should pray:
Our Father in heaven,
may your name be hallowed;
your kingdom come,
your will be done,
on earth as in heaven.
Give us today our daily bread.
Forgive us the wrong we have done,
as we have forgiven those who have wronged us.
And do not put us to the test,
but save us from the evil one.'

The consolation of the blessed will be in the future when God takes up the business of ruling the world. The prayer of the blessed must therefore be for this time to come, and to come quickly. One of the earliest prayers of the followers of Jesus to have survived is *Marana tha*, 'Come, Lord!' It was said in Aramaic in the Greek-speaking church in Corinth (1 Corinthians 16:22) and it was also used in the place where Revelation was written (Revelation 22:17–20).

Matthew believed that Jesus had instructed his followers to pray for God to rule, and this is something that a Jewish teacher of the first century AD would have been likely to do. We know of a prayer (the Kaddish) that was used in synagogue services and included the sanctification of God's name in the world, and the coming of his kingdom in the petitioners' lifetime.

As with Matthew's version of the beatitudes, so also with this prayer, there is careful attention to the Greek wording and this helps us to understand its meaning. The first line is the address: *Our Father in heaven*. Then come three petitions, arranged in identical order of words: the verb is placed first (*hallowed*; *come*; *be done*), then the subject of the verb with the definite article (the *name*; the *kingdom*; the *will*), and after that the possessive pronoun (*your*). You could say that these three lines rhyme in Greek; and just as they have the same structure, so also they mean the same thing: Let God cause his reputation (i.e. his name) to be seen to be holy by beginning to rule, and then his will, and no one else's, will be done.

They are to pray that this will happen, both *in heaven* and *on earth*. Satan and the wicked angels must be cast out of heaven, and the demons and unclean spirits must be thrown into the fires of hell (Matthew 25:41; see also 8:29).

This line of the prayer, *on earth as in heaven*, divides it into two parts: the first part is a reiterated request for God to intervene in the world finally and decisively; the second part is the petition of those who say the prayer for their inclusion in the new world order that is coming, and for this to happen immediately. Hence they say: *Give us today our bread for the morrow* (REB margin); that is: 'Give us now the food of the age to come; let the wedding banquet begin.' For that to happen, we shall have to have been allowed to pass the last judgment, and so we ask that we shall be forgiven just *as we have forgiven those who have wronged us*. We shall also have to be spared the time of testing that is coming on the whole world (Revelation 3:10) when the power of the *evil one* will be greater as the time left for him reaches its close (Revelation 12:12).

The prayer is the cry for help of those who understand the situation they are in. They do not underestimate the dangers that face them; they ask God to act in order that they may go forward into the peace of the age to come. This cry for help is addressed to the one whom the petitioners call their *Father in heaven*. They believe that he will acknowledge them as his children (5:9), and that he will not ignore their prayer but give them what they ask.

We must not think that we can cope.
We believe that you have said that you will act.
Act for us now, or else we shall not survive.

The narrow gate and the wide gate

Matthew 7:13–23

'Enter by the narrow gate. Wide is the gate and broad the road that leads to destruction, and many enter that way; narrow is the gate and constricted the road that leads to life, and those who find them are few.

'Beware of false prophets, who come to you dressed up as sheep while underneath they are savage wolves. You will recognize them by their fruit. Can grapes be picked from briars, or figs from thistles? A good tree always yields sound fruit, and a poor tree bad fruit. A good tree cannot bear bad fruit, or a poor tree sound fruit. A tree that does not yield sound fruit is cut down and thrown on the fire. That is why I say you will recognize them by their fruit.

'Not everyone who says to me, "Lord, Lord" will enter the kingdom of Heaven, but only those who do the will of my heavenly Father. When the day comes, many will say to me, "Lord, Lord, did we not prophesy in your name, drive out demons in your name, and in your name perform many miracles?" Then I will tell them plainly, "I never knew you. Out of my sight; your deeds are evil!"'

Matthew had no illusions: the way that Jesus had taught people to come into God's kingdom would not be popular and few would travel by it. The Sermon on the Mount had begun with the blessing of the poor in spirit, the put-upon, the mourners, and those who longed for justice to be done on the earth. Such bias in favour of the oppressed would not be approved of or welcomed by the majority. The Sermon ends with the piling up of antithetical metaphors: a narrow gate and a wide gate; two roads; sheep and wolves; good fruit and bad; those who build on rock and those who build on sand. It is more likely that we shall be on the wrong side.

It is deeds that count, not words, because words can be merely superficial. The analysis takes us further into recognition of our self-deception. Religious talk can be misleading, and doing all kinds of churchy things with words, such as preaching, exorcising demons or performing miracles, may be only a substitute for what God really requires—doing the will of the heavenly Father.

To find out what that is, the Sermon must be re-read. Matthew often puts the clues at the end of a passage, so that the reader has to go back to the beginning to grasp the sense of it. The will of the Father is: no limit to your goodness; no parading your religion; no short-term rewards of praise and respect; no anxiety and no judgment of others.

The narrow gate means that we shall not be able to enter with any hand-baggage; what we are holding onto will have to be put down, outside, and left there, while we squeeze through. This means getting rid of whatever we cherish and find reassuring: a good reputation; a high opinion of ourselves; a sense of achievement and success. The Sermon on the Mount roots it all out.

Jesus will be led out to crucifixion and a stranger will be compelled to carry his cross for him (rubbing in his failure to persuade any of his disciples to follow him); his clothes will be taken from him, and he will be displayed naked; his last words before he dies will be, 'My God, my God, why have you forsaken me?' (27:46). He will end up with nothing. And this, he will have said, is the way for his disciples also. It did not require much foresight to predict that this could not possibly ever be popular.

> At the narrow gate: nothing to display; no recommendation;
> no feeling good.
> Instead: secret goodness; hidden prayer; concealed
> discipline—and the left hand ignorant of it.
> Help us to drop everything.

Matthew among the sinners

Matthew 9:9–13

As he went on from there Jesus saw a man named Matthew
at his seat in the custom-house, and said to him, 'Follow me';
and Matthew rose and followed him.

   When Jesus was having a meal in the house, many tax-
collectors and sinners were seated with him and his disciples.
Noticing this, the Pharisees said to his disciples, 'Why is it that
your teacher eats with tax-collectors and sinners?' Hearing
this he said, 'It is not the healthy who need a doctor, but the
sick. Go and learn what this text means, "I require mercy, not
sacrifice." I did not come to call the virtuous, but sinners.'

Matthew's Gospel is longer than Mark's because Matthew has
much more of the teaching of Jesus than the earlier Gospel. The
five speeches, for example, are much longer than the
corresponding passages in Mark, and there are more parables in
Matthew than there are in Mark. One might draw the conclusion
that Matthew set a high value on good conduct, and in a way he
certainly did; in his final words, Jesus tells the eleven disciples to
teach the converts to observe all that he has commanded them
(28:20). But in another sense, good conduct does not matter; in

fact, it is a disadvantage. Jesus describes himself in Matthew's Gospel as 'a glutton and a drinker, a friend of tax-collectors and sinners' (11:19).

Matthew himself is described as 'at his seat in the custom-house', and the word for 'custom-house' is from the same root as the word for 'tax-collector'; it means the tax collector's place of work. So, in calling Matthew to follow him, Jesus is inviting into his company, and into the group of the twelve apostles (10:2–4), one of those who are associated in this book with sinners (11:19) and with prostitutes (21:31–32).

There were, moreover, tax collectors and sinners who came to meals in Jesus' house, at his invitation. This surprises the Pharisees: to eat with people is to share their attitudes and way of life. Why should Jesus do this? He answers with a parable: To whom do doctors go, to the healthy or to the sick? And he adds a quotation from Hosea (6:6) in which God says that he looks for mercy, not sacrifice. Jesus is the merciful one, who forgives; the Pharisees are those who present the sacrifice of righteousness, which God does not want. God favours the wicked, and so does Jesus. Why? Tax collectors and prostitutes enter the kingdom of God before the chief priests and elders because what is needed now is not righteousness through keeping the Law, but repentance and faith in Jesus.

Matthew's call illustrates this: he was sitting at his work, which is regarded as immoral, but he is told to follow Jesus; he rose and followed him. No explanation is given, nor was any needed. The readers of this book know that they also are disciples, and that discipleship is a gift they have received. They know too that it is much easier to repent if one is obviously bad; virtue conceals the freedom of God—one might think one had deserved his grace. It is, therefore, a disadvantage to be respectable. Jesus deliberately avoids the good people, the Pharisees, and consorts with the sinners.

Luke added to the saying, 'I have not come to call the virtuous, but sinners', the further words, 'to repentance' (Luke 5:32); and some of those who copied out Mark and Matthew changed the saying in the same way. The unexpected is the original: Jesus does not invite people to repent, but to join his company and eat.

Do not let our respectability mislead us.
The worse we are, the clearer we see the truth.
Thank God for our unsuitability.

Forgiveness

Matthew 9:2–8

Some men appeared, bringing to Jesus a paralysed man on a bed. When he saw their faith Jesus said to the man, 'Take heart, my son; your sins are forgiven.' At this some of the scribes said to themselves, 'This man is blaspheming!' Jesus realized what they were thinking, and said, 'Why do you harbour evil thoughts? Is it easier to say, "Your sins are forgiven," or to say, "Stand up and walk"? But to convince you that the Son of Man has authority on earth to forgive sins'—he turned to the paralysed man—'stand up, take your bed, and go home.' And he got up and went off home. The people were filled with awe at the sight, and praised God for granting such authority to men.

Matthew has abbreviated Mark's account of the miracle, omitting the crowd and the difficulty of getting the sick person to Jesus—how they climbed up onto the roof and lowered him through the ceiling. He has preserved that part of the story that he thought important: people bring someone who is paralysed; Jesus declares forgiveness; scribes think he is blaspheming; Jesus demonstrates the forgiveness by the miracle of healing. Instead of Mark's conclusion: ' "Never before," they said, "have we seen anything like this" ' (Mark 2:12), Matthew has: '[They] praised God for granting such authority to men'. (Note that the word translated 'men' here is the Greek word for human beings, not the other word that means males as opposed to females.)

The reaction of the scribes is caused by the omission of any reference to repentance, good works or any other proof that the man's forgiveness had been prepared for and was deserved. The story contains nothing to say that Jesus had had any dealings with him before; it is simply this: the man is brought; Jesus sees their faith; he says that the man's sins are forgiven; he heals him.

John the Baptist had warned those who came to him for baptism that they must bear the fruit that repentance required (3:7–10); Jesus says very little, in this Gospel, about repentance. (There is some evidence in ancient translations and early quotations for omitting the word at 4:17.) He acted as though God had already forgiven sins; what was needed was faith to believe this, and if you had that faith you would forgive those who sinned against you (see 6:14–15 and 18:21–35).

The sickness that is involved here is paralysis—inability to walk; hence the necessity of bringing the man to Jesus on a bed (or stretcher—something he could be told to pick up and carry away). In scripture, obedience to God is spoken of as 'walking in his ways'; his commandments are a 'road', and the believer 'runs' on it; sin is deviation, leaving the way; Jesus is said by those who flatter him to teach the way that God requires (22:16). A paralysed person cannot run or walk. Sin and guilt incapacitate us. The miracle points to a new life that begins in the faith that everything has been forgiven.

The miracle in Mark had been for the purpose of convincing the scribes that the Son of Man had authority on earth to forgive sins; Matthew glosses this: not only the Son of Man, but human beings generally can tell others that God has forgiven them. No qualifications or limitations are mentioned. No doubt Matthew believed that there were those in the churches who had particular responsibilities (see 16:19 and 18:18), but he says nothing about that here. If God has indeed intended Jesus to declare the universal forgiveness of everyone's sins, then anybody has authority to say so.

Thank you for the forgiveness of sins.
Thank you for the faith of those who carry us to you.
Thank you for those who tell us, 'Your sins are forgiven.'

Take up your cross

Matthew 10:34–39

'You must not think that I have come to bring peace to the earth; I have not come to bring peace, but a sword. I have come to set a man against his father, a daughter against her mother, a daughter-in-law against her mother-in-law; and a man will find his enemies under his own roof.

'No one is worthy of me who cares more for father or mother than for me; no one is worthy of me who cares more for son or daughter; no one is worthy of me who does not take up his cross and follow me. Whoever gains his life will lose it; whoever loses his life for my sake will gain it.'

In chapter 10, Matthew gives us the second section of the teaching of Jesus (the first was the Sermon on the Mount). The occasion is the sending out of the twelve apostles on a mission to preach and heal among the Jews (the mission to all the nations will begin after the resurrection; see 28:19). Though the teaching is appropriate to the missionary situation and to those who are apostles, it is by no means confined to them. It would be a mistake to think that we could ignore it because we were not apostles preparing to preach to Jews.

The appropriateness of the teaching exceeds its context in the narrative. With regard to the passage quoted above, for example, it is the case that all Christ's followers know themselves to be to some extent cut off from those who are not. Jesus causes divisions; it is not the whole truth that he is the prince of peace. A prophesy of Micah is fulfilled:

Son maligns father,
daughter rebels against mother,
daughter-in-law against mother-in-law,
and a person's enemies are found
under his own roof.

Micah 7:6

Matthew was almost certainly a Jew and speaks from his own experience. He and other members of his congregation will have had relatives who have not joined them in baptism and discipleship. There will have been deep and bitter divisions among a people well known for family loyalty. Jesus had even said to a disciple that following him took precedence over burying his father (8:21–22), an obligation usually regarded as the prime duty of a son.

The claims of Christ exceed all others and are paramount; even self-preservation must be abandoned because the followers of Jesus must take up the instrument of their own destruction. This is the first reference to the cross in this Gospel, and it is the cross of the disciple, rather than the cross of Jesus, that is referred to. The expression has been trivialized in Christian devotional usage to mean anything that is inconvenient or distasteful, but in the Roman Empire of the first century it meant the execution of a slave by the occupying foreign power. It was particularly abhorrent to Jews because it involved nakedness; and it reminded them that God had not yet fulfilled his promise that he would give them their own land.

Christianity is not about self-fulfilment, but self-destruction. It offers self-destruction as the way to self-fulfilment: whoever loses his life for Christ's sake will gain it. But losing and gaining are not equal, as if the second cancelled out the first. We cannot follow Christ with the intention of gaining life; that comes under the condemnation of the saying, 'Whoever gains his life will lose it.' In between loss and gain stands the judgment of God, and we cannot control him or fix his decisions for him. God is not mocked.

Help us to learn how to love you more than everything and everyone.
Help us to accept loss and diminishment.
Help us to work against ourselves.

Who is my mother?
Who are my brothers?

Matthew 12:46–50

He was still speaking to the crowd when his mother and brothers appeared; they stood outside, wanting to speak to him. Someone said, 'Your mother and your brothers are standing outside; they want to speak to you.' Jesus turned to the man who brought the message, and said, 'Who is my mother? Who are my brothers?' and pointing to his disciples, he said, 'Here are my mother and my brothers. Whoever does the will of my heavenly Father is my brother and sister and mother.'

One of the dangers of religion is that it may produce minds that are hard and closed. Matthew clearly knew this, and he makes much of it in his book: Jesus condemns the religious leaders, the scribes and Pharisees, for their blindness and lack of sensitivity; they are deceived about themselves (chapter 23). It is, as Matthew well knows, far easier to condemn other people than to criticize yourself. He records a saying of Jesus about a person whose only qualification for removing a speck from someone else's eye is that there is a plank in his own (7:3). Matthew knows there is no limit to the extent to which we can fool ourselves about ourselves.

One form of self-deception that Christian devotion may foster in us is the idea that, had we been contemporaries of Jesus, we would have believed in him and followed him. There is very little support for such an assumption in the Gospels.

The story of the mother of Jesus and his brothers wanting to talk to him may help us to see that perhaps we, too, would have been offended by him. Surely he could have stopped lecturing the disciples for once and been polite to his family for a few minutes?

There is more to the story than that. It attacks something that we (at least in England) hold dear. We love social distinctions and hate levellers. We live by ranking people in order of merit, using various kinds of grading: educational, cultural, economic, athletic and religious. Jesus, however, will not accept that his mother and his brothers have any claim upon his time and attention because they are his mother and his brothers. The only relationship that he acknowledges is through his Father: what counts is doing the Father's will—that and nothing else. This is the basis of association with him, and no exceptions will be made for founder's kin or for anyone else. White Anglo-Saxon Protestants should not think that they can jump the queue.

Jesus is involved in recruiting people who will be associated with him and with his Father. God's plan is to have a family made up of people who are related to him in the closest possible way. But the terms on which he will establish this relationship with himself exclude all the distinctions we make, and by which we set so much store. This is bound to offend us; if it does not, it is because we have not yet realized the implications of it. We have been encouraged by ecclesiastical organizations to accept false ideas of hierarchy and superiority.

The way of Jesus—to the cross—is against all belief in pre-eminence and priority. 'The last will be first, and the first last' (20:16). He will take the lowest place, rejected, condemned, mocked, despised. He will upset us, who want the highest place and admire those who make it there.

Thank you for calling us your brothers and sisters
  and mother.
Forgive us wanting to be first.
Destroy all our ranking systems.

Fruitlessness and fruitfulness

Matthew 13:18–23

'Hear then the parable of the sower. When anyone hears the word that tells of the Kingdom, but fails to understand it, the evil one comes and carries off what has been sown in his heart; that is the seed sown along the footpath. The seed sown on rocky ground stands for the person who hears the word and accepts it at once with joy; it strikes no root in him and he has no staying-power; when there is trouble or persecution on account of the word he quickly loses faith. The seed sown among thistles represents the person who hears the word, but worldly cares and the false glamour of wealth choke it, and it proves barren. But the seed sown on good soil is the person who hears the word and understands it; he does bear fruit and yields a hundredfold, or sixtyfold, or thirtyfold.'

Matthew has now reached a point in his book where he recognizes that an explanation is called for; chapter 13 answers a problem that chapters 1–12 have raised, namely: Why is it that some believe the good news, while others do not? Why does the one gospel produce such different reactions in different people?

Like Mark before him, Matthew turns to the parables of Jesus when his narrative reaches a point where an explanation is needed. The immediate occasion is the appearance of his mother and his brothers: they do not understand, but the disciples do. Why is this?

Exactly the same distinction had been created by the use of parables. Jesus had spoken in parables and some of his hearers had understood him, while others had not. One of the parables explains why this is so. It is the parable of the sower, the seed and the different kinds of ground into which the seed fell. As the parable is told, three parts of it describe how some seeds never bore fruit, and only one part describes the seeds that were fruitful; nevertheless, the figures that are given show that the seeds in the good soil that are fruitful make up for the loss involved in the sowing of the other parts of the field. Marginal deficits do not wipe out overall profitability.

Like Mark again, Matthew provides an explanation of the parable. It is a description of what happens when the good news is proclaimed. There are three hurdles to be overcome: the first is not understanding what is said; the second, lack of endurance; the third, love of other things (they might be described as the devil, the flesh and the world, in that order). There is a limit to how much any parable can correspond with that of which it is a parable: no seed can experience the dangers of path and rocky ground and thistles, but those who hear may pass from one hazard to another. Seeds sown on the path will be eaten by birds in a moment; seeds without root on the rocky ground may last until midday, when the sun scorches them; it will take longer for the thistles to choke the third group; and the final seeds must stay put from sowing till harvest if they are to be fruitful.

As Matthew explains the parable, it is a call to perseverance and a warning of the danger of giving up. There is a subtle balance between what God does and what we must do. The word of the kingdom is the message that comes from God and Christ and inspires joy. But we find that there are rival voices and alternative attractions: we prefer short-term satisfaction to long-term obedience, particularly when that for which we wait does not appear.

The fruitlessness of some seeds will be illustrated in the passion narrative. Jesus will predict that they will all lose faith because of him. Peter will dispute this: 'I never will.' Jesus proves right, not Peter (26:31–35). Nevertheless, in spite of failure, the gospel has borne fruit; the existence of the congregation where Matthew's book is being read proves that there is good soil and a manifold yield.

Give us understanding.
Keep us in the way.
Make us fruitful.

The treasure and the pearl

Matthew 13:44–46

'The kingdom of Heaven is like treasure which a man found buried in a field. He buried it again, and in joy went and sold everything he had, and bought the field.

'Again, the kingdom of Heaven is like this. A merchant looking out for fine pearls found one of very special value; so he went and sold everything he had and bought it.'

Preachers who preach to the same congregation week after week know that they must frequently contradict themselves—and presumably their congregations know it too. Christian faith and Christian life are many-sided, and anything that is asserted must be qualified by a counter-assertion: God's choice and our faith; his grace and our effort; good news and bad news; predestination and freedom; and so on. What needs to be said this week may not be what was appropriate last week, or the fact that something was said last week may make it essential that the opposite be said this week. The truth will lie in holding both together. We know that from Paul onwards, Christianity has never been frightened of contradictions: I, yet not I (1 Corinthians 15:10).

Matthew may strike us as one of those who put most emphasis on obedience to Christ's words. If we look further in his book, however, we shall find examples of the other side of this aspect of the Christian life: he is full of the joy that comes from forgiveness, God's mercy, the happiness that is both unexpected and undeserved.

Some writers on this Gospel have thought that it is the work of more than one author, and have pointed to internal contradictions in the book as evidence of this. But it may be that there is no need to call in such a hypothesis to explain the facts. Perhaps it is that Matthew is the good pastor who recognizes that the truth has many aspects, and that this can only be expressed by paradox. See, for example, a sentence in Thomas à Kempis' *The Imitation of Christ*: 'If you bear the cross willingly, it will bear you' (book 2, chapter 12). In the literal sense, either A is carrying B or B is carrying A: both cannot be true simultaneously. But God's grace and our works are not as easily described.

In the two short parables, the treasure and the pearl, Matthew contrasts the emphasis that there is elsewhere in this book on striving to obey, to do good works, to be fruitful, with two examples of instances where what is received is out of all proportion to what is done to get it. The man who finds the treasure comes upon it by accident, working on land that he does not own; he liquidizes his assets—everything he has: house, furniture, wife, children—to buy the land, so that when he has the treasure he can recover what he has sold and still be immeasurably better off. It is something for nothing through an accident. The pearl merchant, however, is deliberately searching for good pearls; they are his trade and his livelihood. For the sake of one exceptional pearl he will use all his resources because (presumably) he knows that he can sell it for a vast profit.

In both cases, realizing assets is essential to achieving the end, which is wealth. In neither case, however, is there anything to detract from utter joy. Both men are certain of success; they both do the obvious thing. We would congratulate them, do the same ourselves, envy them perhaps.

We are not to be frightened by the narrow gate, the hard road, the total demand of Christ. We do not need anyone's commiseration. All that is required of us is nothing compared with what is offered. It is money for jam.

Sadness would be misplaced.
You treat us too well.
It is everything for nothing.

The way of death and resurrection

Matthew 16:21–23

From that time Jesus began to make it clear to his disciples that he had to go to Jerusalem, and endure great suffering at the hands of the elders, chief priests, and scribes; to be put to death, and to be raised again on the third day. At this Peter took hold of him and began to rebuke him: 'Heaven forbid!' he said. 'No, Lord, this shall never happen to you.' Then Jesus turned and said to Peter, 'Out of my sight, Satan; you are a stumbling block to me. You think as men think, not as God thinks.'

Jesus now announces to his disciples what is going to happen: he must go to Jerusalem and be rejected, killed and raised to life. This prediction will be repeated in chapters 17 and 20, with a further, shorter announcement at the beginning of chapter 26. In these passages there is no explanation of the reason why this is to happen. What is made clear, however, from the way in which Matthew arranges his material, is that the idea of a suffering Christ is unacceptable to his followers. In spite of the warnings, they do not continue with Jesus; they desert him and run away when he is arrested, and Peter disowns him three times.

Peter speaks for all the followers of Jesus when he says, 'This shall never happen to you.' But Jesus says that Peter is now doing what Satan had done in the wilderness: he is tempting Jesus to disobey God; he is thinking human thoughts, not God's thoughts (compare 4:10).

We know from Paul that the first Christian missionaries preached Christ's death and resurrection (1 Corinthians 15:3–11). This was the most important part of the Christian message, and judging from his surviving letters Paul concentrated on this and made very little use of other events in the life of Jesus, or the teaching that he had given.

In the four Gospels, also, the importance of what happened on the final Friday and Sunday is reflected in the proportions of the books and the decreasing pace of the narrative. The main message was: He died and God raised him from the dead.

Crucifixion and resurrection were not expected, and were unacceptable: neither Jews nor Gentiles could see the point.

Christians searched the scriptures to show that they had been prophesied in the past, but they could only do so with the benefit of hindsight: if it had not happened, no one could have worked it out from the Old Testament. Faith comes first, and the belief that it must have been according to the scriptures came later.

However it was that the first disciples came to make sense of what had happened, for later Christians of all ages the way of death and resurrection that Jesus pursued always retains its strangeness. Centuries of teaching, preaching, devotion, writing, music, sculpture and painting have not diminished the shock we feel when we discover that the route we have to go is the same as that along which he went. Nothing ever makes it acceptable. Peter speaks for everybody.

The reason why this is so must lie in the conflict between how we are made and how we are to be re-made. We were made with a powerful will to live, and no doubt we needed it if we were to survive. To be fulfilled, however, we shall have to hand over everything, including the desire to protect ourselves and our lives. Faith is a kind of dying.

Crucifixion and resurrection are more than we can
  cope with.
Forgive us our resistance.
Make us think your thoughts, not ours.

Following

Matthew 16:24–28

Jesus then said to his disciples, 'Anyone who wishes to be a follower of mine must renounce self; he must take up his cross and follow me. Whoever wants to save his life will lose it, but whoever loses his life for my sake will find it. What will anyone gain by winning the whole world at the cost of his life? Or what can he give to buy his life back? For the Son of Man is to come in the glory of his Father with his angels, and then he will give everyone his due reward. Truly I tell you: there are some of those standing here who will not taste death before they have seen the Son of Man coming in his kingdom.'

As early as chapter 4, Jesus had called people to join his company and they had followed him. We are now to see that being with him means more than just being a member of the group; following him involves doing what he does and being treated in the way that he is treated. He has said what this will be in the previous paragraph (16:21–23); he now draws the inevitable conclusion that his followers must travel the same way that he will go.

To understand this passage we need to remember a curious fact about ourselves which, as far as we know, is unique to our species.

We can stand back and be self-critical, approving or disapproving of our actions. We can reflect on ourselves, and plan what to do, either to our advantage or to our disadvantage. It is as if there were two people inside us: the 'I' that thinks and the 'me' that it thinks about.

It is only if we see ourselves in this way that we can make sense of the saying that the followers of Jesus must renounce self. The word 'renounce' (in Greek) will be used later when Jesus warns Peter that Peter will 'disown' him three times (26:34). To renounce or disown is to cut yourself off from another person, to break all links and say that you do not know them. This is what the followers of Jesus must do to themselves: the 'I' that stands back and thinks and plans for 'me' must act as if the 'me' did not exist. I must say, about myself, 'I do not know the man' (26:72, 74).

There is more. It is not only that we must act as if we had no knowledge of ourselves, and live in detachment and dissociation. We must work actively and deliberately against ourselves and aim at our own destruction. Lifting up your cross and carrying it means going to your execution; there is no evidence that it had acquired the weak, metaphorical sense of putting up with inconveniences. If it had, that would be excluded by the words that come immediately after: 'follow me'.

The next saying refers to the situation in which one is sorting things into two groups: what is to be kept, and what is to be thrown away. You must put your life, Jesus says, in with the things to be thrown away; if you put it with the things to be kept, you will lose it. Saving is done by destroying. This is the height of Christian insight.

Our lives are the most precious things we have, because without them we should not be there to have anything. If the choice were between retaining your life and possessing everything else in the world, you would be a fool to choose everything else: you could not enjoy it if you were not around. There is therefore nothing that one can exchange one's life for: it is the essential pre-condition, and it is to be surrendered.

When shall we know whether we have disowned ourselves? Only when the Son of Man comes at the last judgment with his rewards and punishments. Matthew, like most Christians at that time, thought that this would happen soon, while some of those who had been alive at the time of Jesus were still living on the earth.

Not what I want but what you want.
You have made me self-critical: increase my
  self-abandonment.
If you want me, I must let go.

By their fruit

Matthew 11:2–6

John, who was in prison, heard what Christ was doing, and sent his own disciples to put this question to him: 'Are you the one who is to come, or are we to expect someone else?' Jesus answered, 'Go and report to John what you hear and see: the blind recover their sight, the lame walk, lepers are made clean, the deaf hear, the dead are raised to life, the poor are brought good news—and blessed are those who do not find me an obstacle to faith.'

Although Matthew told us that John the Baptist had recognized Jesus as the one who should have baptized him, it is probably reading too much into this later section of the Gospel to create out of it a picture of John, in prison awaiting execution, haunted by doubts as to whether Jesus was his true successor or not. All that the setting (verses 2–3) of the saying of Jesus (recorded in verses 4–6) may mean is that the answer to anyone who asks, 'Is Jesus the one who is to come, or are we to expect someone else?' is, 'Look at what is happening, what you hear and see. People can be recognized by their actions. What do the deeds of Jesus indicate?'

He had laid down the principle at the end of the Sermon on the Mount; he had been warning the disciples there against false prophets and he had said, 'You will recognize them by their fruit' (7:15–20). Now he applies the test to himself: what is the fruit of his work? It is healing for the disabled, life for the dead, good news for the poor. Those who can make the leap to faith in Jesus as God's final agent are blessed: God has revealed to them who Jesus is (compare 16:17).

Why should healing be taken as the key to the question? Why not any of the other activities of Jesus, such as teaching, controversy, appointing apostles or having followers? Part of the reason may be because healing was foretold by the prophet, and the passage that may be in mind here is in the book of Isaiah:

Then the eyes of the blind will be opened,
and the ears of the deaf unstopped.
Then the lame will leap like the deer,
and the dumb shout aloud.

Isaiah 35:5–6

Another reason is because healing is the opposite of Satan's activity: he and his demons are recognized by the deprivation of life that they cause. Jesus is the one who drives out the demons, thus giving life instead of death, and health instead of sickness (see 12:25–28). Those who know how to read the signs of the times will recognize Jesus as the one who proclaims the good news of the coming of God's kingdom: the poor, those who stand to gain most because they have least, are the believers.

Jesus is an obstacle to faith (literally, he causes stumbling) because it is not obvious that he is God's agent, and it never will be, until the end of this age. He will be dismissed as a charlatan, condemned as a blasphemer, crucified with criminals, deserted by disciples, and some will say that his body was stolen in order to deceive people into believing in his resurrection. Faith in him will be one explanation, but only one among others.

The people cured are the evidence. This is, in fact, how it happens in many cases. What impresses us then is the character of the disciples. We believe in him because we believe in them; their goodness points to him.

Thank you for the evidence, the fruit.
Thank you that it is what everyone wants: wholeness.
Thank you that we are better than we should be.

Listen to him

Matthew 17:1-8

Six days later Jesus took Peter, James, and John the brother of James, and led them up a high mountain by themselves. And in their presence he was transfigured; his face shone like the sun, and his clothes became a brilliant white. And they saw Moses and Elijah appear, talking with him. Then Peter spoke: 'Lord,' he said, 'it is good that we are here. Would you like me to make three shelters here, one for you, one for Moses, and one for Elijah?' While he was still speaking, a bright cloud suddenly cast its shadow over them, and a voice called from the cloud: 'This is my beloved Son, in whom I take delight; listen to him.' At the sound of the voice the disciples fell on their faces in terror. Then Jesus came up to them, touched them, and said, 'Stand up; do not be afraid.' And when they raised their eyes there was no one but Jesus to be seen.

In the Gospels of Mark, Matthew and Luke the transfiguration is linked to the first prediction of the passion and resurrection by a note of time: in Matthew, it is 'six days later'. Jesus had told his disciples what would happen to him, and what they must do to be his followers, and this raises the question of his authority: what right has he to say such things? Should we believe him? Should we obey him?

On every occasion in the Gospels when a group of three or four disciples is taken apart from the others something specially important is being revealed. What is revealed in the transfiguration is that Jesus is greater than Moses and greater than Elijah: two of the people who, according to tradition, had not died, but been taken up to heaven while still alive. Jesus is neither inferior to them (because he died), nor to be placed on a level with them: he is greater.

Peter expresses the belief that Jesus is equal to Moses and Elijah when he suggests three shelters, one for each of them. That would put Jesus alongside the Law and the Prophets. But that is not how it is. Jesus is the fulfilment of the Law and the Prophets, not a further addition to them. This is what the voice from the cloud declares, correcting Peter's mistake: Jesus is the unique Son of God, and his followers are to listen to him. What Jesus says may (and will) appear strange, but he has the authority of God to say it.

There is a reference back to what Moses had said to Israel:

The Lord your God will raise up for you a prophet like me from among your own people; it is to him you must listen.

Deuteronomy 18:15

What God had previously said through Moses he now repeats directly. The end of the paragraph matches what the voice has said: they saw no one except Jesus himself alone. His teaching and his presence with them are all that they need.

The terror of the disciples at the sound of the voice from the cloud is understandable. We are not dealing with one with whom we can argue or disagree; we cannot qualify what he says, or distance ourselves from it; he cannot be dismissed as one who belongs to the past. He will say: 'Full authority in heaven and on earth has been committed to me' (i.e. by God, 28:18). This is the one to whom God has told us to pay attention.

Matthew's belief is that Jesus is not only a person who lived in Galilee and Judea in the first century, known to us through the traditions and writings of his followers, but also the one who returned to his disciples after he had been executed and promised to be with them all the days till the end of the age (28:20). Whenever they met, he would be there among them (18:20). An important part of the Christian life must be listening; whatever the problems and practical difficulties, we are required to see ourselves as people who are being spoken to.

Make us listen.
Help us to hear.
Keep us attentive.

The obligations of a bankrupt

Matthew 18:23b–35

'There was once a king who decided to settle accounts with the men who served him. At the outset there appeared before him a man who owed ten thousand talents. Since he had no means of paying, his master ordered him to be sold, with his wife, his children, and everything he had, to meet the debt. The man fell at his master's feet. "Be patient with me," he implored, "and I will pay you in full"; and the master was so moved with pity that he let the man go and cancelled the debt. But no sooner had the man gone out than he met a fellow-servant who owed him a hundred denarii; he took hold of him, seizing him by the throat, and said, "Pay me what you owe." The man fell at his fellow-servant's feet, and begged him, "Be patient with me, and I will pay you"; but he refused, and had him thrown into jail until he should pay the debt. The other servants were deeply distressed when they saw what had happened, and they went to their master and told him the whole story. Then he sent for the man and said, "You scoundrel! I cancelled the whole of your debt when you appealed to me; ought you not to have shown mercy to your fellow-servant just as I showed *mercy to you?" And so angry was the master that he condemned the man to be tortured until he should pay the debt in full. That is how my heavenly Father will deal with you, unless you each forgive your brother from your hearts.'*

Chapter 18 is the fourth section of the teaching of Jesus in this Gospel, and the theme that runs through it is the relationships between members of the Church. It begins with the saying that they must all become like children, and that seems to mean that they are to see themselves as having no rights but only obligations. When children are mentioned in the Gospels (and indeed elsewhere in the New Testament) the primary sense of the metaphor is usually the condition of having no status, owning no property, being without position or experience or skill. A child means a non-person.

To follow Jesus in his passion is to join the company of a criminal condemned to death. He has no right even to life. His followers have to see themselves as no better off than he is.

The parable of the unmerciful servant makes the point. The man who owed ten thousand talents must be a high official, for example, a provincial governor. The sum he owes is huge: it is the product of the largest word for a number (literally, *myriad*) and the highest unit of monetary value (*talent*). His offer to pay in full is implausible; it is a bid for delay. Surprisingly, the king remits the whole debt, simply out of mercy. The far smaller debt that the man's colleague owes to him could easily have been paid, but this is refused, and refused on appeal to justice, instead of mercy. This is what strikes the other servants as so improper. According to a sense of what is right that everyone can acknowledge, the man who had been treated with mercy by his superior (in the case of a large debt) should also have treated his equal with mercy (in the case of a small debt); justice should not have been introduced at all, especially when it would operate to the unmerciful man's advantage. The king's generosity had created an obligation, and the crux of the parable is in the words 'ought you not to have shown mercy...?'

The parable invites us to identify ourselves with the declared bankrupt. If we can see ourselves in him, we shall recognize that we are in no position to press our rights over others. God's mercy to us has cancelled our status and we are like children: we cannot call in the debts that we are owed of respect, honour, gratitude, consideration and so on.

But the problem is that we do not see ourselves as debtors. The notion of owing God anything is not one that we acknowledge. Is this, perhaps, what we have to say?—'we do not see ourselves as we should; we believe that we have good standing with God and that being a creature does not impose obligations on us; like the fool, we say in our hearts, "There is no God." '

Make us see that we are debtors.
Not only debtors, but reinstated, discharged.
We are therefore under obligation to be merciful.

The camel and the needle's eye

Matthew 19:23–26

Jesus said to his disciples, 'Truly I tell you: a rich man will find it hard to enter the kingdom of Heaven. I repeat, it is easier for a camel to pass through the eye of a needle than for a rich man to enter the kingdom of God.' The disciples were astonished when they heard this, and exclaimed, 'Then who can be saved?' Jesus looked at them and said, 'For men this is impossible; but everything is possible for God.'

A man had asked Jesus what good he must do to gain eternal life, and Jesus had replied, 'Keep the commandments.' He had said that he had. What did he still lack? Jesus had replied, 'Sell your possessions; give to the poor; follow me.'

Matthew, in common with his contemporaries in Judaism and Christianity, uses a group of terms without intending any difference of meaning: life, eternal life, the kingdom of heaven, the kingdom of God, being perfect, being saved—all refer to one and the same thing: entry into the age to come.

The man who asked the question had gone away sad because he

was very rich, and the disciples were astonished at what Jesus had replied. It had often been said in scripture that God showed his approval of those who were righteous by rewarding them with success, wealth and prosperity (God did not forsake them, it was thought, and their children did not have to beg for food). If that was how it was, then how could having riches make it hard to enter the kingdom of heaven? And not only hard, but impossible: as impossible as it would be to make a real live camel go through the eye of an ordinary, everyday needle? In fact, it would be easier to do this with a camel than for a rich man to be saved. (There have been many attempts to ease the difficulty of these sayings—wrongly, because it is a mistake to think that Jesus would only have said things of which we can approve.)

The reason why wealth is a bar to entry into the age to come is because it creates an illusion of independence. With it, we are able to get our own way, more or less, preserve our private space, protect our interests, control our time and do what we like. The rich can be independent, as long as their riches last. But this is no preparation for the time when God will rule and his will will be done by all; no private empires will survive. The poor will be better prepared because they will be more accustomed to having their will frustrated. In some manuscripts and ancient translations of the beatitudes, the poor are paired with the meek (5:3, 5), and the meek are those who are put upon by others (especially by the rich). They are the fall guys, the patsies.

God can, however, make exceptions. The only hope for those who are not poor is that God may do the extraordinary and exceptional thing of saving a rich person. But to rely on this is to ask to be treated as an exception; it is to require God to break his own rule and to work overtime to teach us obedience. This is the highly unsatisfactory position that most of us are in.

Why did we think that the way would be easy?
We were warned, frequently.
Let us take nothing for granted.

Final notice to pay

Matthew 21:33–43

'There was a landowner who planted a vineyard: he put a wall round it, hewed out a winepress, and built a watch-tower; then he let it out to vine-growers and went abroad. When the harvest season approached, he sent his servants to the tenants to collect the produce due to him. But they seized his servants, thrashed one, killed another, and stoned a third. Again, he sent other servants, this time a larger number; and they treated them in the same way. Finally he sent his son. "They will respect my son," he said. But when they saw the son the tenants said to one another, "This is the heir; come on, let us kill him, and get his inheritance." So they seized him, flung him out of the vineyard, and killed him. When the owner of the vineyard comes, how do you think he will deal with those tenants?' 'He will bring those bad men to a bad end,' they answered, 'and hand the vineyard over to other tenants, who will give him his share of the crop when the season comes.' Jesus said to them, 'Have you never read in the scriptures: "The stone which the builders rejected has become the main corner-stone. This is the Lord's doing, and it is wonderful in our eyes"? Therefore, I tell you, the kingdom of God will be taken away from you, and given to a nation that yields the proper fruit.'

The parable of the tenants of the vineyard answers the question that a reader of Matthew's book might raise at this point in the narrative: why was it that Jesus was put to death? The parable is based on a passage in Isaiah where the prophet sings a love-song about a vineyard which produces wild grapes instead of the choice variety that had been planted (Isaiah 5:1–7). In Matthew (as also in Mark and Luke) the emphasis is less on the fruit than on the tenants. They should have paid their rent in kind but they have refused to do so. The owner sends two groups of servants and finally his son. The tenants ill-treat the servants and kill the son. Jesus then puts the question, 'How will the owner deal with the tenants after this?' The audience, which is the chief priests and elders, make the obvious reply.

The parable is a thinly disguised allegory: God is the owner, Israel the vineyard, the two groups of servants are the former and the latter prophets and Jesus is the son. The reply of the chief priests and elders is their self-condemnation (and is a feature of the parable only as recorded by Matthew, who seems to have added it to Mark's account of the same incident): God will destroy them and give the vineyard to others, who will pay up—that is, to the Gentiles.

Why, then, was Jesus put to death? The answer given here is that he came in the line of the prophets of Israel, and for the same reason that they came: to summon Israel to obey God. It was thought by some at the time of Jesus that all the prophets had been persecuted (see for example Acts 7:52). Jesus similarly provoked the hatred that caused his death.

He had acted with authority, calling disciples to follow him, appointing the Twelve, proclaiming the coming kingdom, healing the sick, teaching the way that God requires us to live. The greater the authority, the greater the hostility it provokes. To kill the heir will solve the tenants' problem.

No guarantee can be given in advance that a new group of tenants will be any better than their predecessors. There is no reason why the sequence of events in the parable may not be repeated any number of times.

Jesus was put to death because he said what his contemporaries did not want to hear. He came for the rent. He asked for it from those who did not want to see themselves as tenants, and believed they had nothing to pay. We shall not read the passion narrative profitably until we have identified ourselves with the tenants and recognized what it is that we owe.

Remove the veil from our eyes, so that we see you as the one
whom we do not want to meet.
Unstop our ears, so that we can hear what we do not want
to hear you say.
With us, it is either kill him or pay up.

You hypocrites

Matthew 23:23-28

'Alas for you, scribes and Pharisees, hypocrites! You pay tithes of mint and dill and cummin; but you have overlooked the weightier demands of the law—justice, mercy, and good faith. It is these you should have practised, without neglecting the others. Blind guides! You strain off a midge, yet gulp down a camel!

'Alas for you, scribes and Pharisees, hypocrites! You clean the outside of a cup or a dish, and leave the inside full of greed and self-indulgence! Blind Pharisee! Clean the inside of the cup first; then the outside will be clean also.

'Alas for you, scribes and Pharisees, hypocrites! You are like tombs covered with whitewash; they look fine on the outside, but inside they are full of dead men's bones and of corruption. So it is with you: outwardly you look like honest men, but inside you are full of hypocrisy and lawlessness.'

The fifth and last section of the teaching of Jesus in Matthew's arrangement of it is in chapters 23, 24 and 25 of his Gospel. Even the most superficial knowledge of this writer shows us a mind that thinks in pairs of contrasts: good and bad, wise and foolish, edible and inedible, and so on. Matthew had put the beatitudes at the beginning of the first section of teaching (5:3–10). Here, at the beginning of the last section, he puts the opposite member of the pair: alas for those who are not blessed (23:13–33).

Matthew saw hypocrisy in the scribes and Pharisees of his day, but this identifying of wickedness and perversity with specific groups of people was the product of deliberate rabbinical exaggeration, and was not the whole story. It would be a mistake to read this section of Matthew's book in order to have information about the scribes and Pharisees of the latter half of the first century. Those who know most about Judaism at that time tell us that there were good and bad scribes and Pharisees, that they were the people who took God most seriously, and that Matthew is reacting against the Judaism he found himself surrounded by.

Matthew makes it perfectly clear that he knows that we should not judge, and that criticism of other people is the result of greater blindness in oneself (i.e. having a plank in your own eye, 7:1–5). His chapter of woes is best taken as a description of the way in which any religion (including Christianity) can develop. It is also an aid to self-examination, whereby we can check how far we have fallen into the traps that are set for us.

There will always be light and heavy duties—tithing, for example, compared with justice, mercy and good faith. It is easier and more pleasant to perform the former and neglect the latter: to attend carefully to what can be dealt with successfully and to neglect what requires more thought and may never be totally accomplished.

Similarly, there is the subtle temptation to use religion as a form of self-indulgence that satisfies one's own internal needs. Piety on the outside, but the opposite within.

In the third example, religion is used to conceal the truth: the appearance of honesty cloaks corruption. We begin by trying to deceive others, and end up deceiving only ourselves.

It is significant that the woes are addressed to religious people, not to Pilate, the Roman soldiers or those engaged in trade or commerce. The unpleasant fact is that evil finds its most fruitful seed-bed in those who think they have renounced it. Unawareness of self-deception is the best soil for the deadliest sort of wickedness. It is essential to think about this before we come to the passion narrative.

We do resist the truth.
Do not let us deceive ourselves.
Open our eyes to see.

Jesus, his brothers and sisters

Matthew 25:34–46

'Then the king will say to those on his right, "You have my Father's blessing; come, take possession of the kingdom that has been ready for you since the world was made. For when I was hungry, you gave me food; when thirsty, you gave me drink; when I was a stranger, you took me into your home; when naked, you clothed me; when I was ill, you came to my help; when in prison, you visited me." Then the righteous will reply, "Lord, when was it that we saw you hungry and fed you, or thirsty and gave you drink, a stranger and took you home, or naked and clothed you? When did we see you ill or in prison, and come to visit you?" And the king will answer, "Truly I tell you: anything you did for one of my brothers here, however insignificant, you did for me." Then he will say to those on his left, "A curse is on you; go from my sight to the eternal fire that is ready for the devil and his angels. For when I was hungry, you gave me nothing to eat; when thirsty, nothing to drink; when I was a stranger, you did not welcome me; when I was naked, you did not clothe me; when I was ill and in prison, you did not come to my help." And they in their

turn will reply, "Lord, when was it that we saw you hungry or thirsty or a stranger or naked or ill or in prison, and did nothing for you?" And he will answer, "Truly I tell you: anything you failed to do for one of these, however insignificant, you failed to do for me." And they will go away to eternal punishment, but the righteous will enter eternal life.'

This paragraph is the conclusion to the last section of the teaching of Jesus in Matthew's Gospel. Notice how the formula, now to be used for the last time in the book, refers to 'all these discourses' (26:1): it is as if Matthew were saying, 'You have now heard all the Lord's teaching; after this, he goes to his suffering, death and resurrection.'

Jesus is assuring his disciples that he will be with them always, till the end of time. The future second coming does not entail the present absence of Jesus, in Matthew's understanding. Jesus is with his followers both when they are being well treated by those who do not believe in him, and when they are being persecuted by them. Nothing will separate him from them: he rejoices with them and he suffers with them. He will reward those who have treated him and his brothers well, and he will punish those who have not.

The passage answers the question, 'On what criterion will unbelievers be judged?' We have been told that the Son of Man will give everyone his due reward (16:27)—literally, pay everybody according to performance. We have been told also how his servants will be judged: everything depends on what they have done with their talents (25:14–30). But 'everybody' must include those who do not believe: what is the basis of their rewards? It is what they have done to the unknown king's brothers and sisters, and it is as surprising to the righteous as it is to the unrighteous.

There is also here an insight into how the followers of Jesus must see themselves. We are to expect ourselves to be the people who are hungry, thirsty, strangers, naked, ill and in prison; and this is what we would be, if we were following the teaching of Jesus as it is set out in this book. The corporal works of mercy (a medieval list of things a Christian should do) is based on this passage, but as Matthew understands it these are the works that others must do to us, not we to them.

Jesus is about to go to his passion: 'the Son of Man will be handed over to be crucified' (26:2). That is the way in which he saves his people from their sins. His last words to his disciples before the passion narrative begins describe the way in which they must follow him: hunger, thirst, being away from home, nakedness, sickness and imprisonment. This is the way in which they save the unbelievers— providing the occasions for them to do good to the judge and king who is on the earth with his followers. Both for him and for them, the only power they have lies in their powerlessness.

Let us not be ashamed of you and of yours.
Let us not resist dependence on others.
Help us to rejoice in our weakness.

Much from little

Matthew 14:13–21

When he heard what had happened Jesus withdrew privately by boat to a remote place; but large numbers of people heard of it, and came after him on foot from the towns. When he came ashore and saw a large crowd, his heart went out to them, and he healed those who were sick. As evening drew on, the disciples came up to him and said, 'This is a remote place and the day has gone; send the people off to the villages to buy themselves food.' Jesus answered, 'There is no need for them to go; give them something to eat yourselves.' 'All we have here', they said, 'is five loaves and two fish.' 'Bring them to me,' he replied. So he told the people to sit down on the grass; then, taking the five loaves and the two fish, he looked up to heaven, said the blessing, broke the loaves, and gave them to the disciples; and the disciples gave them to the people. They all ate and were satisfied; and twelve baskets were filled with what was left over. Some five thousand men shared in this meal, not counting women and children.

The feeding of the five thousand comes in all four Gospels and it is sometimes said that it is the only miracle story that does. It is not difficult to see why it was so popular: it could be understood in so many ways. There was the eucharist, and it could be regarded as a prefiguration of it; there was the banquet at the end of the world; there had been Moses and the manna at the time of the exodus; and Elisha and the hundred men whom he fed with twenty barley loaves, who ate and left some over (2 Kings 4:42–44). But above all, the story illustrated the deepest conviction of the followers of Jesus that God could make something out of what was almost nothing.

There was no need for the disciples to think that what they had (five loaves and two fish) would not be enough to feed five thousand men, together with women and children. God, who made everything out of nothing when he created the world, can satisfy the hunger of a crowd with very little, and there will be more left over than they had started with to prove it. The story emphasizes the quantities, and the disparity between what one would expect and what is the case. An inadequate supply feeds a huge crowd (Matthew has added 'not counting women and children' to Mark's version in order to underline the size of the number of the people fed), and the number of the baskets of what was left drives the point home even further. Nothing is impossible for God.

It was a lesson frequently taught in scripture that God prefers to work with small numbers in order that people may not think that it is they who have achieved success, but he. He reduces the size of armies (Judges 7), he chooses a small nation rather than a large one to be his people (Deuteronomy 7:7), and he gives victory to David who has no armour and weapons except a sling and a stone (1 Samuel 17). In the same way, what happened to Jesus was not to be dismissed as too insignificant to be important. One more crucifixion of a Jew by Romans might be regarded as nothing more than an extension of a regrettable situation. Matthew and his readers will not agree with that.

To find the action of God we must look in the least expected places, because God takes up what is least to make it great. Abraham, David, a nation that lost its land and a man who lost his life: those were God's starting-points. Much is made out of little; the last become the first; the humble are exalted; life comes from the dead, glory from shame.

Thank you for your power.
Thank you for beginning with the least.
Thank you for not excluding us.

Christ our Passover

Matthew 26:1-5

When Jesus had finished all these discourses he said to his disciples, 'You know that in two days' time it will be Passover, when the Son of Man will be handed over to be crucified.' Meanwhile the chief priests and the elders of the people met in the house of the high priest, Caiaphas, and discussed a scheme to seize Jesus and put him to death. 'It must not be during the festival,' they said, 'or there may be rioting among the people.'

From now until the last day of Lent we shall be reading Matthew's account of the passion of Jesus straight through (chapters 26 and 27) without omissions. The evangelist has already told us how we are to understand this part of his Gospel: disciples must be followers; the way of Jesus is to be our way also. What he did for us in the past he is now doing with us.

Matthew follows Mark closely but makes some small changes, adding details that were not in Mark or omitting some that were. Here in the first paragraph, for example, he has a final prediction of the crucifixion in the direct speech of Jesus, instead of Mark's note of time. Matthew wants his readers to think of Jesus as going to his death voluntarily, knowing all that was to happen to him; he was not caught out by events; he knew what he must do and did it.

The time of the handing over of the Son of Man is significant. It coincides with Passover, when Israel is celebrating the deliverance from slavery in Egypt at the time of Moses and the exodus. That was an act of power accomplished by God through miracles; the Son of Man, on the other hand, will be handed over to be crucified and there will be no miracle to save him. In the previous predictions of these events, both death and resurrection had been mentioned (for example, 16:21); here, it is only his death that Jesus foretells, to emphasize that the way he must go is one of shame, humiliation and powerlessness. The Greek word for 'handed over' will be used fifteen times in these two chapters: of Judas handing Jesus over to the chief priests; of the chief priests handing him over to Pilate; and of Pilate handing him over to those who will crucify him. Jesus becomes the object of other people's actions. His power is exercised in his passivity.

The meeting of the chief priests and elders plans Jesus' death and intends that it should not happen during the festival; there was always a danger of riots when crowds had come in to celebrate Passover. What the authorities were proposing would be overruled by God: Jesus will be arrested during the night of the festival, the very night when Israel came out of Egypt. Christ our Passover lamb will be sacrificed for us (1 Corinthians 5:7).

The whole of Matthew's Gospel has been written out of the faith that what Jesus did and what happened to him were providential. Matthew believed that God was in control, and that that was why scripture was being fulfilled. In the case of the time of the arrest of Jesus, he believed that God's hand could be seen at work: the chief priests and the elders wanted one thing; God wanted another, and what he wanted was what happened. Faith always looks for God in the way things happen, and hangs on to the possibility that he can be glorified, whatever takes place.

Give us faith that nothing is impossible.
Show us how to understand the death of Jesus.
Make us grateful for it.

Giving and getting

Matthew 26:6-16

*Jesus was at Bethany in the house of Simon the leper, when a
woman approached him with a bottle of very costly perfume;
and she began to pour it over his head as he sat at table. The
disciples were indignant when they saw it. 'Why this waste?'
they said. 'It could have been sold for a large sum and the
money given to the poor.' Jesus noticed, and said to them,
'Why make trouble for the woman? It is a fine thing she has
done for me. You have the poor among you always, but you
will not always have me. When she poured this perfume on my
body it was her way of preparing me for burial. Truly I tell
you: wherever this gospel is proclaimed throughout the world,
what she has done will be told as her memorial.'*

*Then one of the Twelve, the man called Judas Iscariot,
went to the chief priests and said, 'What will you give me to
betray him to you?' They weighed him out thirty silver pieces.
From that moment he began to look for an opportunity to
betray him.*

The disciples complain about the waste of the perfume; they are full
of good ideas: sell it and give the proceeds to the needy. We half

expect Jesus to agree with this. It is the kind of proposal that is still to be heard when suggestions are put forward for furnishing and decorating churches: would not the money be better spent on Christian Aid? But Jesus does not agree with the disciples. He defends the woman because she has seen something that they have not appreciated (though they have been told): that Jesus will be with them in the flesh for only a very short time; then, he will be crucified, dead and buried. What the woman has done is to perform the rite of anointing a corpse for entombment. Her good deed will be recalled wherever the gospel is preached (and so, too, will their objection to it).

Jesus' defence of the woman against the displeasure of the disciples is extreme, even, one might say, excessive. He supplies her with a motive she may never have suspected she had. The one who has told his followers not to judge reveals how he will deal with everybody when his time to judge comes at the end of the world: he will provide us with intentions for our deeds that go far beyond anything we ever thought of. This is the love that 'believeth all things'; he will believe us to have been better than we ever thought we were.

With almost unbearable irony, Matthew goes on to describe how one of those who have just been involved in criticizing somebody for wasting her money now goes to the chief priests to ask how much he will get if he hands Jesus over to them. Those who complain about other people's waste are quite capable of making something for themselves out of treachery. Love of money overrides ethical distinctions.

Matthew has added to Mark's account the precise sum that the chief priest gave to Judas. Mark had said that they 'promised him money'. How did Matthew know that it was thirty silver pieces? The most probable explanation is that he alludes to the scriptures: Zechariah had said, 'They weighed out my wages, thirty silver pieces' (Zechariah 11:12).

The life of Jesus must strike those who set much store by efficiency as falling far short of what it could have been. He never wrote anything down for future generations to read; he went to

Jerusalem though he was aware of what would happen there; he had picked disciples who were stupid and cowardly (and one of them a traitor); he rebuked the man who tried to resist his arrest; he did not speak as much as he could have done during his trials before the Jews and the Romans. Why this waste?

We shall not understand Jesus and his passion or our discipleship as long as we think that what matters most is efficiency and success. God is wasteful, and he shows it in the way he runs the world and in the way he redeems it. Both are equally extravagant.

Teach us the love that does not calculate.
Make us givers, not getters.
Convince us that we cannot serve you and money.

Surely you do not mean me, Lord?

Matthew 26:17–25

On the first day of Unleavened Bread the disciples came and asked Jesus, 'Where would you like us to prepare the Passover for you?' He told them to go to a certain man in the city with this message: 'The Teacher says, "My appointed time is near; I shall keep the Passover with my disciples at your house."' The disciples did as Jesus directed them and prepared the Passover.

In the evening he sat down with the twelve disciples; and during supper he said, 'Truly I tell you: one of you will betray me.' Greatly distressed at this, they asked him one by one, 'Surely you do not mean me, Lord?' He answered, 'One who has dipped his hand into the bowl with me will betray me. The Son of Man is going the way appointed for him in the scriptures; but alas for that man by whom the Son of Man is betrayed! It would be better for that man if he had never been born.' Then Judas spoke, the one who was to betray him: 'Rabbi, surely you do not mean me?' Jesus replied, 'You have said it.'

The Passover meal had to be eaten in Jerusalem after sunset, and those who owned houses there let out rooms to pilgrims who had come up for the festival. Matthew gives us no information as to how the arrangements had been made between Jesus and 'a certain man in the city'; he is even less informative on this point than Mark. All the emphasis in the Gospels is on what Jesus said and did at the meal and after. There is no mention of the lamb and the cups of wine that were part of every Passover celebration. To the mind of the Christians, Jesus has taken the place of all Old Testament sacrifice. We recall the voice from the cloud at the transfiguration: 'Listen to him.' Moses and Elijah disappear, and no one is seen except Jesus (17:1–8).

He says that one of the Twelve will hand him over (to his opponents, and eventually to death). They all reject the prediction; one by one they all say, 'Not I, Lord'—expecting the answer, 'No, not you.' But Jesus says it will be one of those who have shared the meal with him. Scripture will be fulfilled and the Son of Man will be handed over. That it was foretold does not reduce the responsibility of the person who does it, because God can work through our choices without violating our freedom; neither the predictions of the Old Testament nor the words of Jesus compel Judas to do what he does. What he does is such that it would have been better for him not to have been born. Matthew goes on to say what Mark had not said, that Jesus identified Judas as the one of whom he was speaking, and we see here again how Matthew wants his readers to know that Jesus was completely aware of what was to happen and accepted it willingly.

Being one of the Twelve, therefore, did not guarantee future blessedness. If what was to happen to Judas was worse than never to have existed, it must, one thinks, be some kind of punishment or torment (see 25:46), and not simply annihilation. Whatever we make of this, that seems to have been Matthew's understanding of what Jesus had said, as it was also Mark's before him.

We are in an area where ideas are difficult to handle and all kinds of speculation are unprofitable. Two points are fairly clear. First, that none of the evangelists knew exactly why Judas had betrayed

Jesus; perhaps he had died before telling anybody. Secondly, it is easy to misjudge oneself. They all said, one by one, 'Surely not I?' and Judas said it again, 'Surely not I?'—even though he had already been paid the thirty silver pieces. If lack of self-confidence is one kind of defect, the presence of too much self-confidence is equally dangerous, perhaps more so. We shall see how none of the disciples comes out of this night without disgrace. There would be no need for us to pray, 'Suffer us not to be separated from thee', unless we thought that we could be. Or to say, 'Lead us not into temptation', if we thought we could resist it. Self-confidence is not enough. What matters is confidence in God and in his Son—that is faith.

Let us not judge others, but ourselves.
Let us not trust ourselves, but you.
Let us never be separated from you.

Take, eat, drink

Matthew 26:26-29

During supper Jesus took bread, and having said the blessing he broke it and gave it to the disciples with the words: 'Take this and eat; this is my body.' Then he took a cup, and having offered thanks to God he gave it to them with the words: 'Drink from it, all of you. For this is my blood, the blood of the covenant, shed for many for the forgiveness of sins. I tell you, never again shall I drink from this fruit of the vine until that day when I drink it new with you in the kingdom of my Father.'

As we have seen, there is no mention of the special features of the Passover meal, but the words and deeds of Jesus at the supper are what interests the authors of the Gospels and their readers. In these four verses (26–29) Matthew gives us an account of what the Lord did and said, and this has always been of the greatest concern to his followers.

Matthew is still reproducing the words of Mark, but with some very slight alterations and additions. For example, he adds the command 'eat', and changes Mark's 'they all drank from it' to another command, 'drink from it, all of you'. He has also added the words 'for the forgiveness of sins', which were not in Mark's account of the supper. It may be possible to understand part, at least, of Matthew's motives in making these changes in the wording of the supper.

The idea of eating someone's body, or drinking someone's blood, would have been extremely hard for Jews to accept. They strictly observed the rule that no blood should ever be consumed, neither of animals nor of humans; and they believed that eating human flesh was totally forbidden. Matthew believed that the Lord had instructed his disciples to do this entirely unexpected thing; and to emphasize it for his readers (many of whom may have been Jews) he includes the two commands 'eat' and 'drink'. His is the only account of the supper that does this (see Mark 14:23–24; Luke 22:17–19; 1 Corinthians 11:24–25).

Jesus is making his disciples perform an action that demonstrates what his relationship to them is to be, and how they are related to him. He says that he is giving himself to them in the form of food and drink. He commands them to consume him, and he tells them that this is part of a covenant that is being made with them, the result of which is the forgiveness of their sins (compare 1:21). Jesus then promises that what is happening in this room on this evening will eventually be fulfilled when the kingdom comes, and then he and all his disciples will eat and drink together in the feast of the age to come.

We saw how in the Lord's Prayer (6:9–13) the disciples were taught to ask for the bread for the morrow, and for the forgiveness of their sins. Now, at the supper, we are assured that both of these petitions will be granted, and this will come about through the death of Jesus, who will never again drink this fruit of the vine, that is, this-worldly wine. Through his death, which will be for them, he will enable his followers to enter the kingdom of his Father, and thus bring about all that the prayer was asking for.

We live by eating and drinking, and this inevitably involves us in destroying: meat, vegetables, fluids. Jesus chooses this essential fact, that is true of all living things, as the way for us to understand his relationship with us. Through this relationship with him, and his death for us, we shall be with him in the kingdom for which we are to pray, 'Our Father...'

Help us to see that we need help.
We depend on you, to come to you.
Jesus says: 'Take. Eat. Drink.'

You will all lose faith because of me

Matthew 26:30–35

*After singing the Passover hymn, they went out to the mount
of Olives. Then Jesus said to them, 'Tonight you will all lose
faith because of me; for it is written: "I will strike the shepherd
and the sheep of his flock will be scattered." But after I am
raised, I shall go ahead of you into Galilee.' Peter replied,
'Everyone else may lose faith because of you, but I never will.'
Jesus said to him, 'Truly I tell you: tonight before the cock
crows you will disown me three times.' Peter said, 'Even if I
have to die with you, I will never disown you.' And all the
disciples said the same.*

The original Greek says simply, 'After singing a hymn they went
out...' The translators of the REB have added the word 'Passover'
because Matthew said that it was the Passover meal that they were
eating (verses 17, 19–20) and part of the observance included
Psalms 114 (or 115) to 118, praising God for deliverance from
enemies.

Pilgrims who had come for the festival were required to stay in

Jerusalem all night, and for this purpose the mount of Olives was considered part of the city.

Jesus predicts the failure of all the disciples: they will lose faith (literally, be scandalized, that is, caused to stumble) because of him. He will be the cause of their lack of faith because his humiliation will make them abandon him; they will not be able to follow him as he has commanded them to do. This will fulfil the prophesy of Zechariah:

> *Sword, awake against my shepherd*
> *against him who works with me.*
> *Strike the shepherd, and the sheep will be scattered,*
> *and I shall turn my hand against the lambs.*

Zechariah 13:7

But this will not be the end, for Jesus or for his followers, because God will act and raise up Jesus from the dead, and he will go to Galilee (where, as we shall see, he will appear to the disciples and send them to all the nations, 28:16–20). We saw during the supper that the life of the disciples depended on Jesus, who related to them as food to be eaten. Here we are shown that there is no way into the kingdom except through death, disaster and restoration by God.

Peter will not accept this. He had disagreed with Jesus before (16:22–23) when he had first predicted his death and resurrection. Now he declares that he will never be made to sin because of Jesus; he will follow him and not fall. All the others may lose faith, but he will be the exception. Jesus replies to Peter that he will certainly be the exception, but not in the way that he expects: he will disown him three times before tomorrow's cock-crow. Peter repeats his assertion of his faithfulness: he would rather die than disown Jesus; and they all say the same.

The disciples have not yet understood the significance of the difference between food and those who eat it: eaters are destroyers. Nor have they understood the prophecy that made the distinction between shepherd and sheep: one is struck, the others are scattered. The ways of Jesus and his followers are about to diverge: he will go ahead to do (and suffer) God's will; they are unable to follow. He must do for them what they cannot yet do with him.

There would be no need for belief in a saviour if we could save ourselves. It is only when we realize that we cannot do so that the need for a saviour becomes clear. In Gethsemane the disciples will learn two lessons: that Jesus accepts God's will for him; and that they cannot do what they are told to do. He is their saviour, and they are those who need his help. They will live off him.

Rid us of false confidence.
Show us our weakness.
Thank you for our failures.

The shepherd and the sheep

Matthew 26:36–50

Jesus then came with his disciples to a place called Gethsemane, and he said to them, 'Sit here while I go over there to pray.' He took with him Peter and the two sons of Zebedee. Distress and anguish overwhelmed him, and he said to them, 'My heart is ready to break with grief. Stop here, and stay awake with me.' Then he went on a little farther, threw himself down, and prayed, 'My Father, if it is possible, let this cup pass me by. Yet not my will but yours.'

He came back to the disciples and found them asleep; and he said to Peter, 'What! Could none of you stay awake with me for one hour? Stay awake, and pray that you may be spared the test. The spirit is willing, but the flesh is weak.'

He went away a second time and prayed: 'My Father, if it is not possible for this cup to pass me by without my drinking it, your will be done.' He came again and found them asleep, for their eyes were heavy. So he left them and went away again and prayed a third time, using the same words as before.

Then he came to the disciples and said to them, 'Still asleep? Still resting? The hour has come! The Son of Man is betrayed into the hands of sinners. Up, let us go! The traitor is upon us.'

He was still speaking when Judas, one of the Twelve, appeared, and with him a great crowd armed with swords and cudgels, sent by the chief priests and the elders of the nation. The traitor had given them this sign: 'The one I kiss is your man; seize him.' Going straight up to Jesus, he said, 'Hail, Rabbi!' and kissed him. Jesus replied, 'Friend, do what you are here to do.' Then they came forward, seized Jesus, and held him fast.

In chapter 17, Jesus had taken Peter, James and John up the mountain and they had heard the voice saying that Jesus was God's only Son; they must listen to him. The same three disciples are now taken aside from the rest, and we see the obedience of the Son to the will of the Father, and the failure of the three to do what they were told. Jesus tells them to stay awake with him, but instead of doing that they fall asleep; and though Jesus wakes them up twice, they still fall asleep for the third time.

The reason why they are to stay awake is in order that they may pray; if they do not pray they will enter into temptation and be unable to resist it. (There is an echo here of words in the Lord's Prayer, 6:9–13.) Jesus comes through the time of testing to accept what the Father has given him to do, but they do not because they have not prayed: they are not prepared for what will happen.

In Greek, one word can mean both to love and to kiss. Judas uses the kiss as the pre-arranged sign by which he will identify the person who is to be arrested. Perversity knows no limits: what should signify friendship is used for the purpose of handing him over to a process that will end in his death.

Matthew has been following Mark word for word through most of this passage, but he adds a sentence to show that Jesus knew what was to happen and accepted it: 'Friend, do what you are here to do.' Judas is the agent through whom God's purpose will be achieved, but this does not annul his responsibility for what he does. It was not Judas' intention to bring about the salvation of the world: what he hoped to do, according to Matthew, was to make money out of the affair.

The story of Jesus and the disciples in Gethsemane encapsulates one aspect of the Church and its relationship to its Lord. It is not so much that we do not know what we should do; we know, but do not do it. The spirit is willing, but the flesh is weak. Jesus is spoken of as the shepherd: he cares for the sheep; and this is how it is with us.

Forgive our repeated failures.
Give us the humility to accept forgiveness.
Thank you for the shepherd's care for his sheep.

Open our eyes

Matthew 20:29–34

As they were leaving Jericho he was followed by a huge crowd. At the roadside sat two blind men. When they heard that Jesus was passing by they shouted, 'Have pity on us, Son of David.' People told them to be quiet, but they shouted all the more, 'Sir, have pity on us; have pity on us, Son of David.' Jesus stopped and called the men. 'What do you want me to do for you?' he asked. 'Sir,' they answered, 'open our eyes.' Jesus was deeply moved, and touched their eyes. At once they recovered their sight and followed him.

Like all experienced pastors, Matthew knows that we deceive ourselves. Religion does not necessarily make us more aware: on the contrary, it may do the opposite and add to our self-delusion. The metaphor that Matthew frequently uses to refer to this is 'blindness'; five times in chapter 23, for example, he says that Jesus referred to the scribes and Pharisees as blind. Here in chapter 20, immediately before Jesus enters Jerusalem, he heals two blind men, restoring their sight, and it is probably the case that Matthew has seen the miracle as the promise of deliverance from self-deception.

The two paragraphs immediately before the miracle (20:20–28) contain the accounts of the request of Zebedee's wife that her sons might sit next to Jesus in his kingdom. Jesus had asked them, 'Can you drink the cup that I am to drink?', and they had said, 'We can.' After that, Jesus had said to the other disciples that the Son of Man would give his life as a ransom for many. Jesus had to drink the cup of suffering first, before his followers could do so. James and John were still under the delusion that there could be private agreements about glory, and that they could do what was necessary. They would have to be humiliated by events before they could see themselves clearly.

In Mark, at the corresponding point in his Gospel (Mark 10:46–52), there was the story of one blind man, Bartimaeus. In Matthew, it is virtually the same story but with two men, and their names are not given. Perhaps the reason why Matthew told his readers about two blind men instead of one was in order to bring out the parallel between the two sons of Zebedee, with their metaphorical blindness, and the two men who were literally blind. Just as the latter followed Jesus, so will James and John, eventually: 'You shall indeed drink my cup.' But only because the Lord, the Son of David, has had pity on them.

Matthew knows all about our ignorance when it is a question of knowledge of ourselves, but he does not want this to make us despair. Jesus, he believes, was put to death because of the blindness of his contemporaries; the followers of Jesus were also being persecuted because of the continuing blindness of those who did not believe. But the condition could be overcome: it did happen that people believed, and it did happen that people understood themselves and, in particular, understood their need for the Son of Man to give his life as a ransom for them. Blindness was not incorrigible. The prayer, 'Open our eyes', should be said with the belief that it would be answered.

Thank you for insight into ourselves.
Thank you for showing us our need of you.
Thank you for faith to follow.

Do not resist evil

Matthew 26:51–56

At that moment one of those with Jesus reached for his sword and drew it, and struck the high priest's servant, cutting off his ear. But Jesus said to him, 'Put up your sword. All who take the sword die by the sword. Do you suppose that I cannot appeal for help to my Father, and at once be sent more than twelve legions of angels? But how then would the scriptures be fulfilled, which say that this must happen?'

Then Jesus spoke to the crowd: 'Do you take me for a bandit, that you have come out with swords and cudgels to arrest me? Day after day I sat teaching in the temple, and you did not lay hands on me. But this has all happened to fulfil what the prophets wrote.'

Then the disciples all deserted him and ran away.

Matthew has added to Mark's account of the arrest of Jesus various sayings that explain why it is necessary for him to give himself up, and why there should be no resistance to those who have come from the chief priests and elders. 'All who take the sword die by the sword': to try to save oneself from destruction by the use of force would be self-defeating. It would be to use evil in order to overcome evil, but the only result of that will be that evil will consume those who have used it. This is certainly how it would have been on that particular occasion: had the disciples resisted the arresting party in Gethsemane, and had Jesus and his followers escaped, the Romans would eventually have caught up with them and rounded them up. Matthew is probably writing his book after AD70, so he can look back on the four years of war with the Romans (AD66–70) that ended in the fall of Jerusalem and an immense death-toll of the Jews.

Matthew, however, draws a universal lesson from this particular occasion: 'All who take the sword…' On the whole, Christians have not followed him in this respect, but have considered there to be occasions when it was right to fight and to use force (for example, for punishment of criminals). Force alone is seldom effective because it breeds resentment and stores up trouble for the future; it has to be accompanied by something else. Even so, one suspects that Matthew took the extreme view, which abandoned the use of force in all situations: 'Do not resist those who wrong you' (5:38–42).

The disciple's sword was unnecessary and inappropriate on this occasion because Jesus is the only Son of the Father and he has unlimited power. To fight to save Jesus is to assume that this is not the case, and to think that God's will can only be done by our intervention. Here again we are faced with an idea that has not been generally accepted by Christians. We do not normally say, when a situation calls for action, 'Leave it to God; he will send his angels to deal with the matter if he wishes.'

Jesus does not appeal to his Father for help because what is to happen (arrest, condemnation, death) is prophesied in scripture. Matthew, like Mark, quotes and alludes to passages in the Psalms and the prophets that relate to the passion. But here again the events had to happen first, before anyone could see that they had been predicted. Discerning the fulfilment of scripture took place retrospectively.

None of these arguments convinces the disciples that they should remain with Jesus. They do not think: 'Force is self-defeating; Jesus could ask for divine aid if he wished; scripture must be fulfilled—therefore we shall stay and suffer with our master.' Only Peter will follow, at a distance; and we know what he will do.

Nothing could convince the disciples of the necessity and rightness of the handing over of Jesus to destruction. This is the moment when the prediction is proved true: 'You will all lose faith because of me' (26:31). But the failure of the disciples is part of the good news: there is unlimited mercy because of the willingness of Jesus to carry the weakness of his followers.

We shall boast of our weakness.
We shall not expect to escape from trouble.
Your will be done.

The unwanted Messiah

Matthew 26:57–68

*Jesus was led away under arrest to the house of Caiaphas the
high priest, where the scribes and elders were assembled.
Peter followed him at a distance till he came to the high priest's
courtyard; he went in and sat down among the attendants, to
see how it would all end.*

*The chief priests and the whole Council tried to find some
allegation against Jesus that would warrant a death sentence;
but they failed to find one, though many came forward with
false evidence. Finally two men alleged that he had said, 'I can
pull down the temple of God, and rebuild it in three days.' At
this the high priest rose and said to him, 'Have you no answer
to the accusations that these witnesses bring against you?'
But Jesus remained silent. The high priest then said, 'By the
living God I charge you to tell us: are you the Messiah, the Son
of God?' Jesus replied, 'The words are yours. But I tell you
this: from now on you will see the Son of Man seated at the
right hand of the Almighty and coming on the clouds of
heaven.' At these words the high priest tore his robes and
exclaimed, 'This is blasphemy! Do we need further witnesses?
You have just heard the blasphemy. What is your verdict?' 'He
is guilty,' they answered; 'he should die.'*

Then they spat in his face and struck him with their fists; some said, as they beat him, 'Now, Messiah, if you are a prophet, tell us who hit you.'

Two events are placed side be side: Jesus before a meeting of the Jewish authorities, and Peter among the high priest's attendants. Jesus is condemned to death for what he says, but Peter escapes with his life for what he says. Matthew tells us that Peter has followed Jesus into the courtyard 'to see how it would all end': he supposes that this is the last he will see of him. Jesus, on the other hand, predicts the exaltation of the Son of Man and his coming on the clouds of heaven to judge the world. One represents unbelief; the other, faith.

The chief priests and those who are with him have already decided what they must do: they must seize Jesus and put him to death (26:4). Having seized him, they need a charge on which to condemn him, and finding that is their present problem.

The different accounts of the trials before the Jews and the Romans in the four Gospels, and the problem of relating these accounts to what is known about Jewish and Roman legal procedures at this time, suggest (as one might expect) that there was little firm information available to the followers of Jesus concerning the events between the arrest in Gethsemane and the crucifixion on the following day. They were there when he was arrested; women were there when he was crucified; but no one knew exactly what had happened in between.

For the tradition that Jesus had predicted the destruction of the temple see 24:2, but notice the difference: Jesus did not say, 'I can pull down the temple...' but, 'all will be thrown down'.

The answer to the high priest's question, 'Are you the Messiah, the Son of God?' is ambiguous: 'The words are yours' (literally, 'You said'); in Mark, at this point, Jesus says: 'I am' (14:62). But his prediction about the Son of Man's exaltation (Psalm 110:1) and coming (Daniel 7:13) are enough to convince the high priest and the others who are present that Jesus had committed blasphemy and should be put to death. The spitting and punching that follow fulfil a prophecy: 'I did not hide my face from insult and spitting' (Isaiah 50:6).

Matthew will have known of similar occasions when followers of Jesus were brought before authorities and condemned to death because of the claims they made for Jesus (see 23:34–36). The most bitter divisions are always those between people who are most closely associated; we become angry when we cannot reach agreement with those with whom we share so much. Jesus and those in the high priest's house would have agreed on many things, but the one issue on which they could not agree was who Jesus was. The question of identity was the cause of his execution.

Keep us asking who you are.
What are you pulling down, and what are you rebuilding?
Help us to understand you.

Whoever disowns me...

Matthew 26:69–75

Meanwhile Peter was sitting outside in the courtyard when a servant-girl accosted him; 'You were with Jesus the Galilean,' she said. Peter denied it in front of them all. 'I do not know what you are talking about,' he said. He then went out to the gateway, where another girl, seeing him, said to the people there, 'He was with Jesus of Nazareth.' Once again he denied it, saying with an oath, 'I do not know the man.' Shortly afterwards the bystanders came up and said to Peter, 'You must be one of them; your accent gives you away!' At this he started to curse and declared with an oath: 'I do not know the man.' At that moment a cock crowed; and Peter remembered how Jesus had said, 'Before the cock crows you will disown me three times.' And he went outside, and wept bitterly.

All four evangelists include the account of Peter denying that he was a follower of Jesus. We might have expected that as the churches looked back to the days of Jesus from later times, they would have had greater respect for his first followers and thought of them as giants of faith, the founder-members of the movement. This is, in fact, what is happening in Matthew's Gospel, and in relation to Peter: it is only here that we have the saying: 'Simon son of Jonah, you are favoured indeed... on this rock I will build my church' (16:17–18). But the tendency to idolize the past and revere apostles as models of virtue did not affect the way in which the story of Peter's three denials was recorded. Matthew follows Mark closely, adding some details the effect of which is, if anything, to increase the enormity of Peter's failure.

Matthew had recorded a saying of Jesus: 'Whoever disowns me before others, I will disown before my Father in heaven' (10:33), and he reminds us of this saying when he comes to tell the story of Peter in the high priest's courtyard: he adds to Mark's account the words 'in front of them all' (using the same Greek word as in 10:33). What Peter does is what has already been explicitly forbidden by Jesus; he has put himself out of the reach of forgiveness: 'I will disown him...' But we know that this is not so; Peter will be among the eleven disciples who see the Lord in Galilee and receive his commission (28:16–20). The sayings of Jesus are not to be interpreted in a pedestrian and legalistic way.

Matthew has also added the words 'with an oath' in verse 72, thus aggravating Peter's guilt; and he has added the explanation that the bystanders recognized Peter as a Galilean by his northern accent (verse 73). The case against Peter piles up.

The prediction that he would fail (26:34) had done nothing to prevent him from doing so; but with the cock-crow comes the recollection of the warning and the increased sense of shame: he has done what he had said he would die rather than do. There is a contrast between the reaction of Peter and that of Judas (in the next chapter): Peter weeps bitterly in penitence, but Judas hangs himself in despair. Compare Paul: 'Pain borne in God's way brings no regrets but a change of heart leading to salvation; pain borne in the world's way brings death' (2 Corinthians 7:10).

Peter's failure is part of the good news because it is an illustration of it: what is to be believed in is the kindness and forgiveness of God, proclaimed by Jesus as he called sinners to be his followers and to share his meals. The very one who is the first of those followers

(10:2) is the one who, after warning, does what is expressly forbidden; he is the best example of what it is about.

Notice how the story is told: it begins in the encounter between the servant-girl and Peter, in the presence of others; then a second girl makes the statement, 'He was with Jesus of Nazareth', to the people there; finally, these people address Peter and point to the clear evidence of his northern origin in his dialect. Peter goes down a slippery slope, making greater asseverations on each occasion, as he gathers speed, reaching the bottom with his curses and oath.

Stop us in our small deceits.
Make us attend to those who warn us.
Thank you for forgiveness.

One God

Matthew 27:1-10

When morning came, the chief priests and the elders of the nation all met together to plan the death of Jesus. They bound him and led him away, to hand him over to Pilate, the Roman governor.

When Judas the traitor saw that Jesus had been condemned, he was seized with remorse, and returned the thirty silver pieces to the chief priests and elders. 'I have sinned,' he said; 'I have brought an innocent man to his death.' But they said, 'What is that to us? It is your concern.' So he threw the money down in the temple and left; he went away and hanged himself.

The chief priests took up the money, but they said, 'This cannot be put into the temple fund; it is blood-money.' So after conferring they used it to buy the Potter's Field, as a burial-place for foreigners. This explains the name Blood Acre, by which that field has been known ever since; and in this way fulfilment was given to the saying of the prophet Jeremiah: 'They took the thirty silver pieces, the price set on a man's head (for that was his price among the Israelites), and gave the money for the potter's field, as the Lord directed me.'

All the evidence points to the death of Jesus by crucifixion, not by stoning—Paul, Mark, the later evangelists and the traditions behind the Acts of the Apostles, Hebrews and Revelation. Stoning was the Jewish method of execution, crucifixion the Roman. There must, therefore, have been some involvement of the Romans in the death of Jesus, and this is why all the Gospels report the handing over of Jesus by the chief priests to Pilate, the Roman governor. (The most recent studies of this subject suggest that the Romans probably played a larger part in the process than the Gospels suggest.)

Mark had said nothing in his Gospel about what happened to Judas after the arrest of Jesus in Gethsemane; he is simply not mentioned again in that book, nor is there anything further about him in John. Matthew and Luke (in the Acts of the Apostles) both tell us that he died, though their accounts differ as to how he did so: in Acts, he fell headlong and burst open so that all his entrails spilled out (1:18); in Matthew, he hanged himself in remorse and despair.

Matthew had included in his account a statement of the sum of money that Judas received from the chief priests, thirty silver pieces (26:15), and we saw that there might have been an allusion the prophecy of Zechariah (11:13). He now returns to that text to tell his readers what happened to the money after Judas had thrown it down in the temple: 'The Lord said to me, "Throw it into the treasury." I took the thirty pieces of silver—the princely sum at which I was paid off by them!—and threw them into the house of the Lord, into the treasury.' This is the Syriac version, but the REB margin tells us that the Hebrew has, instead of 'into the treasury', the words 'to the potter'. Matthew refers to the Zechariah text, but he seems to attribute it to Jeremiah, who visited a potter and bought a field (18:1–3; 32:7–12). Though this is confusing, what is certain is that Matthew believed God had foreseen and predicted these events in the lifetime of Jesus, centuries before they happened; and that nothing had occurred haphazardly.

We can appreciate Matthew's faith, even if we find his application of it problematic. He would not have accepted the idea that God was out-witted by human wickedness; God was totally in control, however human beings behaved. And in particular there was to be no suggestion that Jesus had made a mistake in appointing Judas to be one of the Twelve; it had all happened in order that scripture might be fulfilled.

Paul had said that there is no limit to the faith that love produces (1 Corinthians 13:7). If we are to love God with all our heart and soul and mind (22:37), we shall have to think that he will have everything in his control, eventually; that he is reliable and cannot be thwarted; that he is the beginning and ending, alpha and omega.

We believe in one God.
Teach us to trust you.
Everything is in your control.

Jesus Barabbas or Jesus called Messiah?

Matthew 27:11–18

Jesus was now brought before the governor; 'Are you the king of the Jews?' the governor asked him. 'The words are yours,' said Jesus; and when the chief priests and elders brought charges against him he made no reply. Then Pilate said to him, 'Do you not hear all this evidence they are bringing against you?' but to the governor's great astonishment he refused to answer a single word.

At the festival season it was customary for the governor to release one prisoner chosen by the people. There was then in custody a man of some notoriety, called Jesus Barabbas. When the people assembled Pilate said to them, 'Which would you like me to release to you—Jesus Barabbas, or Jesus called Messiah?' For he knew it was out of malice that Jesus had been handed over to him.

Pilate asks Jesus, 'Are you the king of the Jews?' but Matthew does not explain how he came to do so. He may have assumed that his readers would understand that this was the charge that the chief priests and elders had decided upon, with which to ask for execution (27:1). Like Mark, Matthew will make much use of the title 'king of the Jews' in his account of the crucifixion (verses 29, 37, 42); unlike Mark, Matthew has prepared us for it in the earlier parts of his book (1:6–16; 2:2; compare also 21:5). Both evangelists believe that Jesus is seen most clearly as king when he is being put to death; it is by giving up his life that he exercises authority; by serving us, not by lording it over us (see 20:24–28).

When charges against Jesus are made, he is silent; he does not speak in his own defence or explain who he is, either to his accusers or to the governor who has the power to put him to death. This surprises Pilate: normally, people on trial are keen to argue against their opponents. Matthew's readers, however, know that this is a time not to speak: the scriptures must be fulfilled (for example, Isaiah 53:7); the will of the Father must be done; and in any case no explanations will be effective with those have already decided what the outcome will be (see 27:1).

Outside the Gospels, there is no evidence that Roman governors released prisoners at festivals; if it was the custom, one might have expected the Jewish historian Josephus to have mentioned it. The incident makes the death of Jesus a matter of choice, and Pilate puts the alternatives to those who are assembled: 'Which do you want? Jesus or Barabbas?'

In Matthew, according to some manuscripts (followed here by the translators of the REB), but not in the other Gospels, Barabbas (the name means 'Son of the Father') also had the name Jesus. Hence Pilate's question is, 'Do you want Jesus Barabbas, or Jesus called Messiah [i.e. Christ]?' (The name Jesus, which is the Greek form of the name Joshua, was common in Judaism in the time before the Christian era.) Pilate knows which they will choose because he understands the intentions of the Jewish authorities: they want Jesus destroyed, therefore they will ask for the notorious prisoner Jesus Barabbas to be released. Their motive is malice (or, as it might be translated, 'envy').

Both men are called Jesus, which means saviour (see 1:21), and whichever of the two dies, he will save the other from death. Both men are Sons of the Father: one by nature (as every man is), the other by the power of the Holy Spirit (see 1:20). One is the agent of God, sent by him into the world to fulfil God's promises and be Messiah; we know nothing about the other, except that he was in custody and a person of some notoriety. The safe choice is Barabbas because he is less troublesome; he would be the favourite, chosen by most committees charged with the responsibility of selecting a candidate for an appointment.

You have put before us two ways.
We believe that we are free to choose.
Help us to choose rightly.

Pilate and the people

Matthew 27:19–26

While Pilate was sitting in court a message came to him from his wife: 'Have nothing to do with that innocent man; I was much troubled on his account in my dreams last night.'

Meanwhile the chief priests and elders had persuaded the crowd to ask for the release of Barabbas and to have Jesus put to death. So when the governor asked, 'Which of the two would you like me to release to you?' they said, 'Barabbas.' 'Then what am I to do with Jesus called Messiah?' asked Pilate; and with one voice they answered, 'Crucify him!' 'Why, what harm has he done?' asked Pilate; but they shouted all the louder, 'Crucify him!'

When Pilate saw that he was getting nowhere, and that there was danger of a riot, he took water and washed his hands in full view of the crowd. 'My hands are clean of this man's blood,' he declared. 'See to that yourselves.' With one voice the people cried, 'His blood be on us and on our children.' He then released Barabbas to them; but he had Jesus flogged, and then handed him over to be crucified.

The account of the decision that Jesus should be crucified is longer in Matthew's Gospel than in Mark's. Matthew has the message from Pilate's wife about her dream, the hand-washing and the people's acceptance of responsibility for the death of Jesus—none of which was in Mark. Up to this point in his passion narrative he has not made many additions to Mark, but he has here. Why?

Two factors may be suggested to explain these additions. First, the Christian movement in the first century found the Roman officials far less hostile to them than the members of the synagogue. Certainly this is the picture in Acts: the Jews cause the trouble, while the magistrates attempt to keep the peace. The only exceptions, in the first century, were the persecutions of Christians in Rome at the time of Nero, in the sixties, and a possible repetition at the time of Domitian, in the nineties, but this is uncertain. Secondly, the destruction of Jerusalem in AD70, at the end of the Jewish war, seems to have been interpreted by some Christians as punishment for the crucifixion of Jesus and persecution of his followers. (See, for example, 22:1–14 and note verse 7: 'The king was furious; he sent troops to put those murderers to death and set their town on fire.')

Matthew's additions to Mark's account of the condemnation of Jesus may be the result of his intention to present the Romans as unwilling to take part in what happened, and to blame it all on the Jews: they took responsibility upon themselves and their children.

Post-1945 research on this subject tends to go in the opposite direction: to exonerate the Jews (except perhaps for the chief priests and their advisers) and to see the Romans as attempting to avoid rioting which (they feared) could have been started by someone proclaiming the kingdom of God in Jerusalem at Passover. The four evangelists progressively whiten Pilate and blacken the Jews; but in fact it was the other way round.

The anti-Jewish theme runs all through Matthew's book, largely in passages that have been added by the evangelist to his source (Mark): for example, in the contrast between Herod and the astrologers; in John the Baptist's condemnation of the Pharisees and Sadducees in the section on the rejection of Jesus and the

Twelve (chapters 11 and 12); and in the chapter of woes (23). It reaches its peak here with the words that Matthew has put into the mouths of 'all the people': 'His blood be on us and on our children.' Living after the Holocaust, inevitably we are more acutely aware of the problem of racism than our predecessors.

Religious differences have led to persecutions, wars and mass slaughter, but Jesus goes to his death silently and without cursing those who demanded his crucifixion—even in Matthew's account of it. It is his followers who have blamed the Jews and often treated them as people who have no rights in society because (it is said) they accepted responsibility for the death of God's Son. One result that might come from this disastrous history of fear and intolerance, in which Matthew's Gospel has played some part, is that we may learn from it that there is a better way to treat people whose faith is different from our own. Variety rather than uniformity seems to us the way in which God is pleased to be worshipped (we no longer think it appropriate to burn our opponents). Another consequence is that we accept the value of historical and critical study of religious documents: it is thanks to that that we can read Matthew and recognize his intentions.

We have made mistakes.
Help us to see your goodness in those with whom
* we disagree.*
Not my will, but yours.

Hosanna to the Son of David

Matthew 21:14–17

In the temple the blind and the crippled came to him, and he healed them. When the chief priests and scribes saw the wonderful things he did, and heard the boys in the temple shouting, 'Hosanna to the Son of David!' they were indignant and asked him, 'Do you hear what they are saying?' Jesus answered, 'I do. Have you never read the text, "You have made children and babes at the breast sound your praise aloud"?' Then he left them and went out of the city to Bethany, where he spent the night.

The description of the blind and the crippled coming to Jesus in the temple to be healed, and of the boys shouting 'Hosanna to the Son of David', is not in Mark but has been added by Matthew. It is probably another example of Matthew's method: he seeks to draw parallels with the (Old Testament) scriptures in order to portray Jesus as the fulfilment of those scriptures.

One of the clues here is the expression 'the blind and the crippled'. It came three times in 2 Samuel 5:6–8, the description of David attacking the Jebusites and taking the stronghold of Zion, the city of David. The Jebusites had said, 'You will never come in here, not till you have disposed of the blind and the lame'; and David had exhorted his troops to kill 'the lame and the blind, David's bitter enemies'. Matthew sees Jesus as unlike David his ancestor: David used force, but Jesus is the healer. David became king in Zion by war, Jesus is king by being crucified there.

This reversal is recognized by children; that is, by those who have not yet learned the ways of the world. Matthew is drawing on another passage from scripture, and this time it is from the Psalms:

You have made children and babes at the breast
sound your praise aloud.

Psalm 8:2 (Greek translation)

Those whom we would expect to recognize God's agent, the chief priests and scribes, are indignant at what is happening; those whom we would not expect to understand are praising God for what is happening. Compare 11:25, 'I thank you, Father, Lord of heaven and earth, for hiding these things from the learned and the wise, and revealing them to the simple' (literally, to 'babies', the same word that is translated 'children' in verse 16).

What anyone might have expected God's final agent to do is the opposite to what in fact he did; and it took people who had no qualifications to see it as the work of God. Cleverness can spoil things. Simplicity sees more clearly and acknowledges goodness, as it also smells out sham and hypocrisy. The children in the temple in Matthew's Gospel fill the same role as the child in the story of 'The Emperor's New Clothes': adults are taken in; the young speak the obvious truth. Jesus is not acting like David; he is healing whereas David was destroying.

Thank you for the insight of the simple.
Thank you for revealing yourself in goodness.
Thank you for rejecting our cleverness.

A king mocked

Matthew 27:27–31a

*Then the soldiers of the governor took Jesus into his residence,
the Praetorium, where they collected the whole company
round him. They stripped him and dressed him in a scarlet
cloak; and plaiting a crown of thorns they placed it on his
head, and a stick in his right hand. Falling on their knees
before him they jeered at him: 'Hail, king of the Jews!' They
spat on him, and used the stick to beat him about the head.
When they had finished mocking him, they stripped off the
cloak and dressed him in his own clothes.*

The evangelists do not describe the physical suffering of a person
being crucified, nor do they invite us to share the pain of Jesus as a
way for us to identify ourselves with him. They wrote for those who
saw people being crucified, so they did not need to describe the
process; nor was it represented in paintings or sculpture for many
generations. Instead of this, the evangelists concentrated on the
mental suffering of Jesus, caused by mocking.

Jesus is mocked by the Roman soldiers: he is dressed in a
soldier's red cloak, crowned and given a sceptre; they kneel to him
as to the emperor and address him as king. (The same word was

used in Greek for 'emperor' and 'king'.) But it is all done in jest: the crown is made of thorns; the sceptre is a stick; they spit on him and use the sceptre to hit him on the head.

Matthew and his readers believe that Jesus is the king of the Jews; this adds a further element to the situation. He is not being mocked for what he is not, but for what he is. He was descended from David along the line of the kings of Judah, and he was addressed as son of David. He is what he has been condemned for claiming to be—the Messiah; but he reveals who he is by being rejected and crucified. The sceptre, which is a symbol of a king's power, is used to strike him on the head; his power is his ability to suffer and to refuse to use power.

Evil triumphs over good, but this is the way that evil is overcome. Its apparent success is its undoing. Jesus has aligned himself with the Father's will, and his suffering will absorb and destroy what overcomes him.

Here Matthew employs irony: he uses language so that it means one thing to one group of people, and another to those who are in the know. The soldiers mean: 'You are not a king or an emperor. You are a person condemned to death and soon to die. You cannot lead an army against Rome. We are in charge here, not you. We hit you with your sceptre. We spit in your face.' Matthew's readers are in the know, and they believe that Jesus is the one to whom God is about to give all authority in heaven and on earth; he will come as judge of the world, and king; he will sit on a glorious throne; he will be accompanied by all the angels. All this is to happen because he has not resisted arrest, not argued his way out of condemnation, but surrendered to the will of the Father.

Faith changes the signs, making pluses into minuses and minuses into pluses. What looks like humiliation is glory; power in powerlessness.

Give us faith to understand humiliation.
Teach us the blessedness of being insulted.
Stop us from justifying ourselves.

For us and for our salvation

Matthew 27:31b–34

Then they led him away to be crucified.

On their way out they met a man from Cyrene, Simon by name, and pressed him into service to carry his cross. Coming to a place called Golgotha (which means 'Place of a Skull'), they offered him a drink of wine mixed with gall; but after tasting it he would not drink.

Jesus had said to his disciples, 'Anyone who wishes to be a follower of mine must renounce self; he must take up his cross and follow me' (16:24). But by now all the disciples have deserted him and run away (26:56), and Peter has sworn an oath that he is not a follower of Jesus (26:69–75). So there is no disciple left to carry the cross willingly and somebody must be compelled to do it, pressed into service by the Roman soldiers. (The word used here is the same as the word used of compelling a person to go one mile, 5:41.) Matthew abbreviates Mark's account at this point (see Mark 15:21), but he retains the name of the man who was involved: it was Simon; not Simon son of Jonah who had refused to believe that Jesus must be crucified (16:17, 22), but another man of the same name, from Cyrene on the North African coast. What Jesus is to do, he is to do for everybody: therefore no one can go with him voluntarily. The compelling of a stranger draws attention to the absence of a disciple; and the fact that both were called Simon underlines the point.

Matthew alters details that were in Mark's account of the drink that was offered to Jesus before he was crucified. Mark had: 'They offered him drugged wine, but he did not take it' (15:23); Matthew has changed this to: 'They offered him a drink of wine mixed with gall; but after tasting it he would not drink' (27:34). As Mark records this, the intention of those who offer the drink is probably to relieve pain; but Matthew finds the fulfilment of a passage in the Psalms—it is Psalm 69:21 (in the Greek translation):

They gave me gall for my food
And for my thirst they gave me vinegar to drink.

In Mark, Jesus refused the anaesthetic; in Matthew, he tastes it first and then refuses. The Psalm is fulfilled more exactly.

The effect of these detailed changes in the way in which the passion is described is to create in those who hear it an atmosphere of mystery and reverence. This is no ordinary day; what is happening on it will change things until the end of time. We have to imagine those who first heard the Matthew passion as people who knew some of the scriptures at least very well indeed. All they needed was a single word to signal a passage in the Psalms or elsewhere that they had heard before. Such a word is *chole*, 'gall', which is only used in its literal sense here in the New Testament; it could create the attitude: 'God told us long ago that this would happen.'

The proper response to Matthew's account must, therefore, include such ideas as: this was meant to be; Jesus was doing the Father's will; it was for us and for our salvation that he did it; when we were weak, Christ died for us; we are embraced by the love of God.

You went to Golgotha for us.
We were helpless, sinners, enemies.
One died for all.

The last temptation of Christ

Matthew 27:35-44

When they had crucified him they shared out his clothes by casting lots, and then sat down there to keep watch. Above his head was placed the inscription giving the charge against him: 'This is Jesus, the king of the Jews.' Two bandits were crucified with him, one on his right and the other on his left.

The passers-by wagged their heads and jeered at him, crying, 'So you are the man who was to pull down the temple and rebuild it in three days! If you really are the Son of God, save yourself and come down from the cross.' The chief priests with the scribes and elders joined in the mockery: 'He saved others,' they said, 'but he cannot save himself. King of Israel, indeed! Let him come down now from the cross, and then we shall believe him. He trusted in God, did he? Let God rescue him, if he wants him--for he said he was God's Son.' Even the bandits who were crucified with him taunted him in the same way.

In these ten verses Matthew refers to Psalm 22 three times (and once again, in the paragraph that follows; see 27:46). The soldiers sharing the clothes by casting lots refers to verse 18 of the Psalm:

They shared out my clothes among them
and cast lots for my garments.

The passers-by wagging their heads and jeering recalls verse 7 of the Psalm:

All who see me jeer at me,
grimace at me, and wag their heads.

And the words of the chief priests, scribes and elders: 'He trusted in God, did he? Let God rescue him if he wants him,' are a quotation from verse 8:

'He threw himself on the Lord for rescue;
Let the Lord deliver him, for he holds him dear!'

The writer of Psalm 22 is describing the conflict between faith and unbelief: unbelief mocks faith because faith will continue to trust, even when there is no longer any evidence to support it. Unbelief concludes that faith is mistaken as soon as the evidence weakens.

If the faith is that God cares for those who trust him, then the crucifixion is, according to the opponents of Jesus, the clear evidence that he is not God's Son. The temptation of Jesus, at the beginning of the book, had raised the problem of God's care for the one whom he had declared his Son: would he not feed him in the wilderness? Would he not support him if he jumped from the temple? Now the religious authorities raise the same problem, attributing to Jesus what the voice from heaven had said at the baptism: 'This is my Son.' They say, 'He said he was God's Son.'

Matthew has replaced Mark's note of time ('It was nine in the morning when they crucified him', 15:25) with the statement that the soldiers sat down there to keep watch. Matthew uses his Gospel to answer charges made against Christians by their opponents (see 27:62–66; 28:11–15). It may be therefore that the reason why Matthew says that the soldiers kept guard over Jesus until he had died was that someone said that he had been removed from the cross while still alive. This was impossible, Matthew asserts, because the soldiers guarded him (see also 27:54.)

It was the custom to exhibit a notice on or near a cross stating the crime that the condemned man had committed. Matthew expands Mark's 'The King of the Jews', to 'This is Jesus, the king of the Jews'. The intention of the notice was to warn people against committing the same crime. Here it is saying, 'This is what happens to people who think they are kings.' But the irony is that Jesus is king by not using force; that he saves others by not saving himself; and that there would be nothing worth believing if he did come down from the cross—only that God can intervene when he wants to, and what comfort would that be to those who suffer when he does not?

The presence of the bandits, on the right and left, may refer to a prophecy of Isaiah:

He exposed himself to death
and was reckoned among transgressors.

Isaiah 53:12

The word translated 'bandits' was used of 'freedom-fighters' or 'nationalists'.

The religious leaders and the bandits taunt Jesus. They both want evidence of power, and they have both abandoned faith as the way of God. They have sided with unbelief in Psalm 22, and left Jesus as the sole representative of faith which is committed unconditionally.

Jesus is mocked by the religious people and those who are
*   politically active.*
What do we expect from God?
Though he slay me, yet I will trust in him.

The stumbling-block

Matthew 27:45–54

From midday a darkness fell over the whole land, which lasted until three in the afternoon; and about three Jesus cried aloud, 'Eli, Eli, lema sabachthani?' which means, 'My God, my God, why have you forsaken me?' Hearing this, some of the bystanders said, 'He is calling Elijah.' One of them ran at once and fetched a sponge, which he soaked in sour wine and held to his lips on the end of a stick. But the others said, 'Let us see if Elijah will come to save him.'

Jesus again cried aloud and breathed his last. At that moment the curtain of the temple was torn in two from top to bottom. The earth shook, rocks split, and graves opened; many of God's saints were raised from sleep, and coming out of their graves after his resurrection entered the Holy City, where many saw them. And when the centurion and his men who were keeping watch over Jesus saw the earthquake and all that was happening, they were filled with awe and said, 'This must have been a son of God.'

Matthew continues to reproduce Mark's account and to make small additions of his own: here, he adds the earthquake, the opening of the graves and the appearance of the resurrected saints in Jerusalem—none of which was in Mark's Gospel. The final words of the section, literally, 'Truly this was the Son of God', spoken now by the centurion and his men, may have a rather different meaning in Matthew from what they had in Mark.

Matthew wants to assure his readers that Jesus has done and suffered all that was required of him. This unexpected and extraordinary event was meant to take place. When Israel came out of Egypt, the last two plagues were the three-day darkness over all the land of Egypt and the death of all the first-born (Exodus 10:21–23 and 11); now there is darkness over all the land (presumably of Israel) for three hours and it is God's Son who dies. The last words of Jesus are the beginning of the Psalm (22) that had been referred to three times in the previous paragraph; Jesus has become the one who speaks the Psalm, the one whose faith is tested by means of total destruction. The mocking of the religious leaders has convinced him of his complete abandonment by God. 'Eli' is similar in sound to the Greek form of the name Elijah (Elias); the prophet was believed to be in heaven, taken up in a whirlwind (2 Kings 2) and ready to help those in distress. The 'sour wine' is another reference to Psalm 69:21, where the same word is used in the Greek version: 'For my thirst they gave me sour wine to drink.' Elijah does not come; he had returned as John the Baptist, and been put to death by Herod and Herodias (14:3–12; 17:10–13).

The tearing of the temple curtain from top to bottom is to be understood as a sign from God, but Matthew does not pause to explain its significance: possibly he thought that it signified God's wrath with those who had sought the death of Jesus. The resurrection of the saints and their appearance in Jerusalem after Jesus' resurrection (only in Matthew's Gospel) point to Jesus as the first fruits from the dead.

Mark had passed directly from the death of Jesus (and the tearing of the temple curtain—out of sight of those at the crucifixion) to the statement of the centurion (literally): 'Truly this man was the Son of God'. If it was meant to be a confession of faith, it was not clear how Jesus' death—as described by Mark—had led the centurion to believe. Matthew is aware of the difficulty. He changes what is said and introduces the miracles that convinced not only the centurion but also his men. He changes Mark's 'truly this man', which might have been disparaging (meaning 'this fellow'—'he really was the Son of God: of course not!') to 'this', making the statement into a confession of faith—of Gentiles, rather than Jews.

Although Matthew has introduced an earthquake (here and again in 28:2), the appearance of resurrected saints and the faith of the soldiers, he has retained Mark's description of the death of Jesus in circumstances of the greatest distress and desolation. (Unlike Luke, he has not altered the final words of Jesus; see Luke 23:46.) Matthew knows that there is an insoluble problem: why does God allow this to happen to his Son? To anybody? For all the suggestions he has made—the fulfilment of scripture; the will of the Father; the forgiveness of sins—he knows that the gospel of Christ's death remains a stumbling-block to everybody, even to those who think they can understand it with their heads. Rational explanation does not dissolve the problem. Matthew leaves the story to make its own impression on those who hear it.

We do not understand.
Keep us believing it is for us.
Give us the thanks to thank you for it.

Waiting

Matthew 27:55–61

A number of women were also present, watching from a distance; they had followed Jesus from Galilee and looked after him. Among them were Mary of Magdala, Mary the mother of James and Joseph, and the mother of the sons of Zebedee.

When evening fell, a wealthy man from Arimathaea, Joseph by name, who had himself become a disciple of Jesus, approached Pilate and asked for the body of Jesus; and Pilate gave orders that he should have it. Joseph took the body, wrapped it in a clean linen sheet, and laid it in his own unused tomb, which he had cut out of the rock. He then rolled a large stone against the entrance, and went away. Mary of Magdala was there, and the other Mary, sitting opposite the grave.

After all the jeering and shouting in the earlier part of the day, Matthew's final paragraph has no direct speech. Silence follows the centurion and his companions' confession, 'This was the Son of God.'

There are no male followers of Jesus to carry the narrative forward because they have all lost faith, as Jesus had said (26:31);

but there are many women who had seen to Jesus' needs in Galilee, and three are mentioned by name: Mary of Magdala (not referred to previously in Matthew), Mary the mother of James and Joseph (presumably the mother of Jesus; see 13:55), and the wife of Zebedee, who was also the mother of James and John (see 20:20–21). Matthew, like Mark, whom he is copying here, may have had another Psalm in mind:

My friends and companions shun me in my sickness,
and my kinsfolk keep far off.

Psalm 38:11

Compare Matthew's 'from a distance' (the same words in Greek).

Like others in the ancient world, Jews attached great importance to the decent burial of the dead; and each evangelist reports that the corpse of Jesus was dealt with in the proper way. (Mark had said that there was no time for anointing the body and that that was why the women came on Easter Day; nevertheless, the woman at Bethany had done it in advance, Mark 14:8. Matthew leaves out the statement that the women came to anoint the body: in his narrative the tomb was sealed. They came, therefore, to see it.)

The man who sees to the burial is called a disciple of Jesus, by Matthew, and a rich man, perhaps referring to Isaiah 53:9 (RSV).

They made his grave with the wicked
and with a rich man in his death.

It was a *clean* linen sheet, Matthew says, and it was an *unused* tomb; and the entrance was closed by a *large* stone. The two Maries sat opposite—they can bear witness that the body that was put into the tomb was the body of Jesus, and that no deception was perpetrated.

Matthew arranges the stage for what he is to tell us in the remaining pages of his book: the stone was sealed; a guard was set; God raised Jesus from the dead and he was seen and touched by the women before he appeared to the remaining eleven disciples in Galilee. But Matthew says nothing at all to enable his hearers to enter into the minds of the women at this time—and he does not mention the men. Proper body disposal was attended to, but as to the minds of the characters, we are given no help for thinking their thoughts. He had said earlier, of Peter, 'He sat down... to see how it would all end' (26:58); the only thing for the women to do is to return to look at the grave (28:1).

The Christian religion provides its followers with no information about life after death. Will there be a time of waiting? What will happen next? Can we picture eternal life? We are in the position of people waiting without knowing what they are waiting for. What will happen will be more that we can imagine. Hope is for what we cannot see.

You keep us waiting.
We do not know what we are waiting for.
Only that we wait for you.

The guarded tomb

Matthew 27:62–66

Next day, the morning after the day of preparation, the chief
priests and the Pharisees came in a body to Pilate. 'Your
excellency,' they said, 'we recall how that impostor said while
he was still alive, "I am to be raised again after three days."
We request you to give orders for the grave to be made secure
until the third day. Otherwise his disciples may come and
steal the body, and then tell the people that he has been raised
from the dead; and the final deception will be worse than the
first.' 'You may have a guard,' said Pilate; 'go and make the
grave as secure as you can.' So they went and made it secure
by sealing the stone and setting a guard.

The account of the guard at the tomb is in Matthew's Gospel and
none other; nor is there anywhere, in first-century writings,
Christian or non-Christian, any reference to it. For example, no one
is recorded as saying to the Jewish authorities, 'You know perfectly
well that he was raised from the dead; the tomb was guarded, and
the guard told you what happened.'

The story is probably the result of controversy between the
followers of Jesus and those who did not believe. When the disciples

preached the resurrection, others replied saying his body had been stolen by his followers. The followers answered with the story of the guard: 'We could not possibly have removed the body: the tomb was sealed and guarded.'

The chief priests and the Pharisees (mentioned here for the first and last time in Matthew's passion narrative) describe Jesus as an imposter, and refer to the time 'while he was still alive'. This is the only place in the New Testament where the verb 'to live' or the noun 'life' are used of Jesus with reference to the time before his death. The custom among his followers was to say that he had died and was now alive; his life began after his death. But here it is the unbelievers who are speaking, hence the unusual expression.

The final deception, they say, would be worse than the first: by 'the first' they mean faith that Jesus was sent by God as prophet, Messiah, God's only Son; the 'final deception' would be to believe in his resurrection, which would be seen as God's authentication of him. Pilate agrees to their request because he does not want a riot any more than they.

None of the other three evangelists attempted to describe the resurrection; they all believed that it happened while no one was there. The earliest writer we know of to attempt a description is the pseudonymous author of the Gospel of Peter (probably mid-second century). Inevitably people asked how it had happened: they had asked similar questions about their own resurrection as early as the time when Paul was writing his letters (1 Corinthians 15; 1 Thessalonians 4:15—5:11). Of all the New Testament writers, Matthew comes nearest to writing an account of what happened because he tells us there were people at the tomb all the time, from Saturday morning to Sunday at daybreak; and not only the women who had followed him, but also guards, who were independent witnesses and could not be accused of having been deceived by the impostor. The guards, who were introduced to prevent belief in the resurrection, in effect witness the earthquake, the descent of the angel and the rolling back of the stone. The passion narrative had begun with a plan to arrest Jesus 'not during the festival', and it went wrong; it comes to an end with another plan, to prevent belief in resurrection, and that also fails.

Lying behind Matthew's story is the conviction that God is not mocked, and that no one can frustrate his purposes. No amount of planning, organizing, guarding against eventualities could ever defeat his plans. Our mistaken attempts to preserve things as we think they should be only play into his hand, and our unbelief furthers his truth.

> *Confound our politics.*
> *Frustrate our knavish tricks;*
> *On thee our hopes we fix:*
>   *God save us all.*

I will be with you always

Matthew 28:1–20

About daybreak on the first day of the week, when the sabbath was over, Mary of Magdala and the other Mary came to look at the grave. Suddenly there was a violent earthquake; an angel of the Lord descended from heaven and came and rolled away the stone, and sat down on it. His face shone like lightning; his garments were white as snow. At the sight of him the guards shook with fear and fell to the ground as though dead.

The angel spoke to the women: 'You', he said, 'have nothing to fear. I know you are looking for Jesus who was crucified. He is not here; he has been raised, as he said he would be. Come and see the place where he was laid, and then go quickly and tell his disciples: "He has been raised from the dead and is going ahead of you into Galilee; there you will see him." That is what I came to tell you.'

They hurried away from the tomb in awe and great joy, and ran to bring the news to the disciples. Suddenly Jesus was there in their path, greeting them. They came up and clasped his feet, kneeling before him. 'Do not be afraid,' Jesus said to them. 'Go and take word to my brothers that they are to leave for Galilee. They will see me there.'

While the women were on their way, some of the guard went into the city and reported to the chief priests everything that had happened. After meeting and conferring with the elders, the chief priests offered the soldiers a substantial bribe and told them to say, 'His disciples came during the night and stole the body while we were asleep.' They added, 'If this should reach the governor's ears, we will put matters right with him and see you do not suffer.' So they took the money and did as they were told. Their story became widely known, and is current in Jewish circles to this day.

The eleven disciples made their way to Galilee, to the mountain where Jesus had told them to meet him. When they saw him, they knelt in worship, though some were doubtful. Jesus came near and said to them: 'Full authority in heaven and on earth has been committed to me. Go therefore to all nations and make them my disciples; baptize them in the name of the Father and the Son and the Holy Spirit, and teach them to observe all that I have commanded you. I will be with you always, to the end of time.'

It is now widely thought that Mark's Gospel originally ended at 16:8, where the women flee, trembling with amazement, and say nothing to anyone. Whether that was the intended ending or not, Matthew seems to have had no more of Mark 16 than those eight verses. Everything from Matthew 28:9 onwards has been added on by him.

He had to make some changes in order to continue the story, as we can see in Matthew 28:8, where the women are not silent through fear (as in Mark) but run to bring the news to the disciples with great joy.

There are two appearances. One is to the women, and it is not only an appearance, they clasped his feet. The other is to the Eleven, in Galilee, where Jesus declares the authority he has received from God, commands them to make disciples of all nations, baptizing and teaching, and promises to be with them till this age ends and he comes in judgment. (Compare the similar ending in 2 Chronicles

36:23: Cyrus has authority; he sends Jews to Jerusalem; he prays that the Lord be with them.)

The final words of the book recall the prophecy that was quoted at the beginning of it: 'He shall be called Emmanuel, a name which means "God with us".' Notice that there is no account of an ascension into heaven, as in Luke and Acts; Jesus is to be thought of as present, not exalted to God's right hand; suffering with his disciples, as he promised in 25:31–46. When they meet in his name, he is there among them (18:20); Matthew's book is read and expounded, and his followers hear his commands and believe his promises.

Thank you for Matthew's Gospel.
Thank you for the resurrection.
Thank you for Christ's presence.

Appendix I

(See Introduction page 10)

The following diagram may help to provide a way of
seeing Matthew's arrangement of the five teaching
sections of his book:

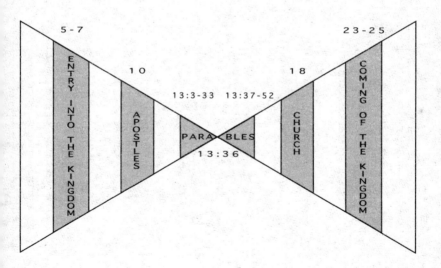

Appendix II

(See Introduction page 11)

The plot of the book may be set out as follows:

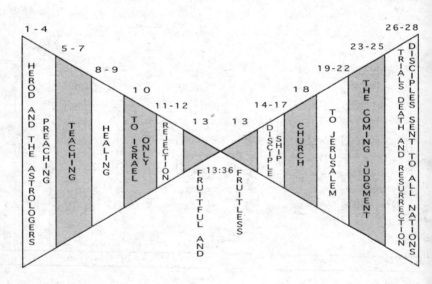

Appendix III

(See page 17)

The women in the Matthean genealogy

Exceedingly odd is the means by which God
Has provided our path to the heavenly shore—
Of the girls from whose line the true light was to shine
There was one an adulteress, one was a whore:
There was Tamar who bore—what we all should deplore—
A fine pair of twins to her father-in-law,
And Rahab the harlot, her sins were as scarlet,
As red as the thread that she hung from the door;
Yet alone of her nation she came to salvation
And lived to be mother of Boaz of yore—
And he married Ruth, a Gentile uncouth,
In a manner quite counter to biblical lore:
And of her there did spring blessed David the King,
Who walked in his palace one evening and saw
The wife of Uriah, from whom he did sire
A baby that died—oh, and princes a score:
And a mother unmarried it was too that carried
God's Son, and him laid in a manger of straw,
That the moral might wait at the heavenly gate
While sinners and publicans go in before,
Who have not earned their place, but received it by grace,
And have found them a righteousness not of the law.

M.D. Goulder, *Midrash and Lection in Matthew*, S.P.C.K., 1974, page 232

Notes for group meetings

First group meeting (after Ash Wednesday)

For this first meeting, it helps if all the members of the group have been asked in advance to read the Introduction to this book (pages 8 to 14), and if it is known that the main purpose of the meeting on this occasion will be to discuss points that the Introduction has raised.

One suggestion made there (page 9) was that we would understand Matthew's book better if we read it straight through from beginning to end, if possible at a single sitting. (And it would be even better, if we did this more than once.) Has anyone tried to do this? What difficulties did they find? What impressions did the book make when read in this way?

A Gospel has been described as a text to be performed. It may be that it will be appreciated best if it is listened to, while somebody else reads it aloud. It would almost certainly take too long to read the whole Gospel in this way at a group meeting, but one of the sections of teaching (see page 10) can be read to the group by a member who has had time to prepare it.

One of the questions that may come up at this point is the way in which the first three Gospels agree with one another and the suggestion that one writer has copied from another. For parallel passages in Matthew and Mark, compare Matthew 9:1–17 with Mark 2:1–22, for example, and notice both the similarities and the differences.

Other questions that may be asked concern: the use of the Old Testament in Matthew's Gospel; anti-Jewishness; references to hell; and the celebration of weakness and poverty. These are all topics to which we shall return later during the course of Lent. There will be other opportunities to think about them, but it may help if someone makes a note now to do this later.

Second group meeting (after first week of Lent)

A question that may arise now is to do with who Jesus is. Matthew and his contemporaries clearly thought this very important, and attempts to produce a clear definition of the Lord occupied the Church for three and more centuries; it was the cause of bitter controversies. But does it matter? What do we make of the attitude, 'It does not matter who he is; what matters is what he said and what he did?'

Another question concerns the meaning of the expression 'the kingdom of heaven'; and it may help if the group looks up two passages in Daniel (chapters 2 and 7) where the stone and one like a human being (Son of man) are symbols of God's rule. What do we make of this way of thinking about the future (i.e. apocalyptic)?

Do we find the Beatitudes (Matthew 5:3–10) attractive or do they present a picture that we dislike?—a wet or a wimp? Does Christianity need to change the image of what the followers of Jesus should be like?

Probably the whole of a session could be spent in thinking about the Lord's Prayer, said so often in churches. What do we mean when we say it?

Third group meeting (after second week of Lent)

It will almost certainly be necessary to allow plenty of time to discuss the meaning of the saying of Jesus: 'No one is worthy of me who does not take up his cross and follow me' (Matthew 10:38). In what ways are we meant to be our own executioners? Is it not perverse (or perverted) to think that we can have joy through the loss of our lives? How should we 'follow Jesus' in today's world? What does losing your life for Christ's sake actually mean for us?

Fourth group meeting (after third week of Lent)

How are we to obey the command, 'Listen to him?' How does Jesus speak to people today? How do we know that it is he who is speaking, and not our own thoughts that we are hearing? Does the principle 'You will know them by their fruit' help us here?

Can we help one another to understand the parable of the debtor? Some may find it an easier way to understand themselves than others do. This raises the whole question of guilt and forgiveness, and almost everybody is grateful for further explanation.

It is sometimes said that Jesus did not say that *all* his followers should sell everything; only one man. Is this so? And if it is not, what do we make of this passage (Matthew 19:23–26) today when it is generally assumed that poverty is an evil to be eliminated from society?

Would it be true to say that if we did not find the sayings of Jesus hard to accept, it would be because we had not heard what he was saying?

How can we best deal with our own self-deception? Are there any aids for seeing ourselves as others (and God) see us?

Which is more blessed, to give or to receive?

Fifth group meeting (after fourth week of Lent)

It might help some members of the group if time was set aside to discuss why we are spending about three weeks concentrating on the passion narrative. Have Christians got their proportions right? Or is this attention to the suffering and death of Jesus excessive and distorted?

What is the place of extravagance in the Christian life? Is it not surprising that Jesus defends the woman with the perfume?

The group will probably want to discuss Judas Iscariot and his betrayal of Jesus, and one question that may be raised here is, 'Why do we know so little about Judas, about what he thought he was doing and why he did it?' Is it that we do not *need* to know?

Another topic that could profitably be discussed this week is, 'What is the meaning of the words of Jesus at the Supper; and what does the communion service mean to us?'

Also; Is it right to think that we need a saviour, or should we be more self-reliant?

Sixth group meeting (after fifth week of Lent)

What are we to make of the attitudes of Jesus to force, as it is described in Matthew's Gospel? How does this apply to us today?

Jesus is presented to us as one who pulls down and rebuilds; does this provide us with a clue to the answer to the question, 'What is he doing in our time?'

A question that might be considered is, 'Why is the account of Peter's three denials of Jesus in all four Gospels? Why is it good news? Would it not be kinder to Peter not to keep on about it?'

Is it possible to believe that God has everything in his control, so that he can be loved and thanked, whatever happens? (See, for example, the first two chapters of Job.)

What do we make of the description of the leaders of the Jews in Matthew's Gospel?

Seventh group meeting (after Holy Week)

Does it help to explain the differences betwen Matthew and Mark in the account of the crucifixion, if we think of the Gospels as primarily writings that are to be read to a congregation at the time of worship: they proclaim the good news so that by hearing them read there may be faith? Does it explain the differences between them, if we think of the aim of the writers as, in the first place, to promote faith, rather than simply to provide information?

Are there any situations in which thinking about the crucifixion of Jesus helps us to believe in God? Is the cross illuminating, so that we can see our path more clearly because of it?

What difference has Good Friday made to the world? What if Jesus had come down from the cross?

Eighth group meeting (after Easter Sunday)

The most important point to notice may be the difference between the last chapter of Matthew and the last chapter of Luke (also the first chapter of Acts). Matthew does not refer to the Ascension of Jesus into heaven. Jesus does not go away from his disciples but (just the opposite) he remains with them. These are his last words in the book, and we are not meant to think that when he had said them he left his disciples.

Matthew's book is to be read in the light of this promise with which it ends; then it will be found that it describes the Lord who is with us, and what it is he is here to do: he assures us of the rule of God; he teaches us how to enter it; he heals us so that we can walk in God's ways; he carries us, suffering with us and for us.

If we understand Matthew's Gospel in this way, does it help to make sense of it? Do the positive benefits of the book outweigh the problems that it raises?

Can we thank God for Matthew?

If you have enjoyed reading *The Matthew Passion*, you may wish to know that BRF produces two regular series of Bible reading notes published three times a year (in January, May and September). *Guidelines* contains commentary and reflection on the Bible, arranged in weekly sections, with a devotional 'Guidelines' section each week. *New Daylight* contains daily readings with printed Bible passages, brief comments and prayers, and is also available in a large print version.

Copies of *Guidelines* and *New Daylight* may be obtained from your local Christian bookshop or by subscription direct from BRF (see over).

For more information about *Guidelines*, *New Daylight* and the full range of BRF publications, write to: The Bible Reading Fellowship, Peter's Way, Sandy Lane West, OXFORD OX4 5HG (Tel. 01865 748227).

SUBSCRIPTION ORDER FORM

Please send me the following, beginning with the Jan/May/Sep* issue:
*delete as appropriate

Qty

_____	Guidelines	£9.00 p.a.†	_____
_____	New Daylight	£9.00 p.a.†	_____
_____	New Daylight large print	£12.00 p.a.†	_____

All prices include postage and packing.

Please complete the payment details below—all orders must be accompanied by the appropriate payment—and send your completed order to **BRF, Peter's Way, Sandy Lane West, Oxford OX4 5HG.**

Name . . . .

Address . . . .

. . . . Postcode . . . .

Signed. . . . . Date . . . .

Payment for subscription(s)   £ _____

Donation   £ _____

Total enclosed   £ _____

Payment by cheque ☐ postal order ☐ Visa☐ Mastercard☐

Expiry date of card . . . .

Signature . . . .
(essential if paying by credit card)

BRF is a Reg. Charity (No. 233280)   TMP

NB _New Daylight_ and _Guidelines_ may also be obtained from your local Christian bookshop—ask at your local shop for details.
† Prices quoted are for subscriptions beginning May 1996 issue.